"Brenda Marie Davies brings important truths to the long, complicated history and intersection of sexuality and spirituality. She is a sex-positive Christian, and her journey in *On Her Knees* is a must-read for anyone struggling to reconcile their faith with their orgasm."

— Liz Goldwyn
author, filmmaker, and founder of The Sex Ed

"Brenda has the courage to talk about a topic that most others either won't touch or distort through the lens of purity culture—and she does so with strength, knowledge, vulnerability, clarity, and authenticity. Not all will cheer her on, but they will have to listen."

— Peter Enns
author of *How the Bible Actually Works* and *The Sin of Certainty*

"Davies's story reads like something out of our sacred text: a narrative full of humanness, complexity, and faith. By telling us about her life and what she has learned, she carves out even more space for a spiritual life in the grey, inviting us to see that no matter what we have been told there is room for the holy in our sensuality."

— Hillary L. McBride
author of *Mothers, Daughters, and Body Image:*
Learning to Love Ourselves as We Are

"What Brenda does in *On Her Knees* is expose the all-too-common story of what happens when power corrupts faith communities. It's a hard look at how the bad theology inherent in evangelicalism is lived out in our actual bodies. And, better still, Brenda is showing us all a better way to be followers of Jesus in the here and now. Said another way: the bitch can preach. Read her book."

— Kevin Miguel Garcia
author of *Bad Theology Kills: Undoing Toxic Belief and*
Reclaiming Your Spiritual Authority

"In this honest—and at times raw—memoir, Brenda Marie Davies leaves behind the god she calls Purity to rediscover the God of love. With searching candor and open-heartedness, Davies writes about the damages she suffered from purity culture and her path into greater authenticity, compassion, and faithfulness. *On Her Knees* is both a compelling read and a thoughtful companion to anyone on her own journey of desire and temptation."

— Natalie Carnes
author of *Motherhood: A Confession*

"There's a lot of imagined, wished for, regrettable, forgettable sex—and body talk, and bawdy talk—in this memoir, but it's absolutely not *sexy*. Davies has a sexual story only a former fundagelical could write—where body and spirit have come completely and tragically untethered from one another. That's not what the church intended, but it's what the church has wrought for lots of us. God help us get ourselves put back together. Stories like this should help."

— KATIE HAYS
founder and lead evangelist of Galileo Church and
author of *We Were Spiritual Refugees*

"Brenda Marie Davies has had an extraordinary life, and yet there is nothing extraordinary about her efforts to overcome the shame of evangelical purity culture. Fear of God's punishment, guilt about sexual desire, and self-blame are themes that resonate for anyone who has struggled with the exacting toll of sexual purity. Written with candor and grace, Davies's unique story holds truth for so many of us who are seeking to find unity between our bodies and our souls."

— SARA MOSLENER
director of the After Purity Project and
author of *Virgin Nation: Sexual Purity and American Adolescence*

"I used to think you were either happy or sad. There was right and wrong, good and evil, black and white. You were a believer or you weren't. But then life happened. Brenda leaves the comfort of what she's expected to believe, who she's expected to be, and in the chasm between expectation and lived reality, and with a perfectly imperfect journey, she courageously steps outside cultural and religious norms and into the immense grey. In the space between, she discovers a God more loving, healing, and expansive than the flattened version she learned about in Christian purity culture. Davies boldly shares her story, shame free, and contagiously invites us to dig deeper into our stories, beliefs, and narratives about love, sex, God, and who we believe ourselves and others to be. No matter who you are, what you do or don't believe, there is an invitation for you in this book as you encounter God in the grey."

— KAT HARRIS
author of *Sexless in the City* and host of *The Refined Collective* podcast

"As a fellow spiritual refugee of the religious abuse known as purity culture, I found Brenda's memoir at times oddly familiar—although at times notably much more star-studded and juicier than my own life. In the vacuum that re-mained after leaving her evangelical, patriarchal concepts about sex behind, she struggles to find a new morality, a new sexual ethic, that honors her convictions, her desires, and her sense of agency. Brenda deconstructs the toxic theology she inherited with honesty and raw humor and unearths for the reader something precious in its wake: grace."

— ELLE DOWD
preacher, activist, educator, and author

"Davies journeys from evangelical Christian purity culture to Hollywood at its hottest—making pit stops at the Playboy Mansion and backstage with Marilyn Manson—as she struggles to reclaim a sexuality that has been squeezed, suppressed, used, and abused to meet the disparate desires of men. In the process, the young woman who spent most of her life on her knees—be it for a rock-and-roll god or a religious one—learns to stand up for herself. Hers is a story with which many young women, forced to reconcile the world's incongruous expectations for their sexuality, will identify."

— LINDA KAY KLEIN
author of *Pure: Inside the Evangelical Movement That Shamed a Generation of Young Women and How I Broke Free*

"Behind the walls of fear, shame, and opprobrium, Eros always seeks a way through the cracks. Brenda Marie Davies is that rare brave soul who trusted the instincts of her desire. Now, with *On Her Knees*, she looks back on those walls and cleaves open those cracks, so that others, like her, might find their way out of the shadows and into a place of sexual authenticity and self-integration."

— IAN KERNER
sex therapist and *New York Times* bestselling author of *She Comes First*

"In *On Her Knees*, Brenda Marie Davies exposes the lies of evangelical purity culture that have long crushed the spirit and ruined the lives of millions of faith-filled Christians. This brave and honest story exposes the experience of thousands like her who have suffered the debilitating shame of the patriarchal purity movement. In contrast, stubborn and resilient explorers like Brenda, who listen instead to the quiet voice of their hearts, offer an alternative. They hear the true loving voice of God. It is a voice calling them toward truth, calling them toward love, and calling out the abuse of power that has long been the tradition of patriarchal Western empire religion."

— TINA SCHERMER SELLERS
author of *Sex, God, and the Conservative Church: Erasing Shame from Sexual Intimacy*

"*On Her Knees* is no flimsy summer 'beach read.' No, it's the kind of book that grabs you by the shoulders and makes you think. In this book, Brenda Marie Davies takes readers on a guided tour of conservative Christian purity culture that will leave them haunted. With the precision of a surgeon, she vividly explores the way purity culture distorts the way people view bodies, sex, and the Divine. From the carnage of an evangelical hellscape, Davies offers hope for self-acceptance, healing, and, dare I say, salvation."

— JONATHAN MERRITT
contributing writer for *The Atlantic* and
author of *Learning to Speak God from Scratch*

"Refreshing and honest, *On Her Knees* provides a soothing antidote to all of us who grew up in the shame-addled world of purity culture and a shocking, unfiltered anecdote to those who did not. A vital and necessary work for one and all, no matter your upbringing."

— KAREN MAINE
writer and director of *Yes, God, Yes*

"Reclaiming spirituality after the loss of religion is a complex, and often painful, journey. For many of us, what feels most frightening is that we believe we are doomed to take that journey alone. But in her profoundly candid memoir, *On Her Knees*, Brenda Marie Davies offers herself to all of us as both sister and mother, companion and guide. Let this book wash over you like a baptism—a stunning reminder of the holiness of your entire being."

— JAMIE LEE FINCH
author of *You Are Your Own: A Reckoning with
the Religious Trauma of Evangelical Christianity*

ON HER KNEES

Memoir of a Prayerful Jezebel

BRENDA MARIE DAVIES

WILLIAM B. EERDMANS PUBLISHING COMPANY
GRAND RAPIDS, MICHIGAN

Wm. B. Eerdmans Publishing Co.
4035 Park East Court SE, Grand Rapids, Michigan 49546
www.eerdmans.com

Published 2021
Printed in the United States of America

27 26 25 24 23 22 21   1 2 3 4 5 6 7

ISBN 978-0-8028-7853-3

Library of Congress Cataloging-in-Publication Data

Names: Davies, Brenda Marie, 1983– author.
Title: On her knees : memoir of a prayerful Jezebel / Brenda Marie
     Davies.
Description: Grand Rapids, Michigan : William B. Eerdmans Pub-
     lishing Company, 2021. | Includes bibliographical references. |
     Summary: "A coming-of-age story about a fervently religious
     Christian woman moving to Los Angeles and rejecting the sex-
     ual mores of her youth"—Provided by publisher.
Identifiers: LCCN 2020046885 | ISBN 9780802878533
Subjects: LCSH: Davies, Brenda Marie, 1983– | Christian bi-
     ography—California—Los Angeles. | Sex—Religious
     aspects—Christianity.
Classification: LCC BR1725.D3595 A3 2021 |
     DDC 277.308/3092 [B]—dc23
LC record available at https://lccn.loc.gov/2020046885

To my spiritual pillars, Mom and Dad
To Kris, for his unconditional love
To David, our seer and protector
To my party boy, babe Valentine
To Rose
And to the God is Grey community, without whom
none of this would be possible

CONTENTS

CONTENTS

ACT 3

FOREWORD

This book is deeply unsettling.

It's like reading the story of the prodigal son set in modern-day LA.

But instead of a son, it's the story of a beautiful blonde girl.

And instead of glossing over the details of her time away from home, she shares the unvarnished story of her partying, and sexual adventure, and exploration, and heartache.

This is a testimony unlike any you've heard because it's so honest. Brenda refuses to repent of learning, and failing, and even blesses her rebellion for what it taught her about life, pleasure, and real faith.

What will upset the tightly wound religious more than anything is her insightful critique of the stifling, spiritless, dead church that she left behind. Brenda doesn't pretend that everything was roses and rainbows back home. This legalistic, "elder-brother religion" is not what she returns to—it's what she comes back to dismantle and reform.

I know a lot about elder-brother, dead religion because I bought into it and propagated it most of my life. When I was twenty-one, I wrote a book called *I Kissed Dating Goodbye*—a book that shaped the purity culture of the evangelical church and that harmed Brenda and so many others who read it.

When I finally came to grips with the damage and harm my book caused and denounced it, Brenda was someone who extended friendship and grace to me. I think people who know real grace are best able to give it to others.

What unsettled me personally from Brenda's story was her ability to hold on to her faith and her love for Jesus in the face of all the pain and harm she experienced in the church. Most days I find it easier to just walk away from it all. Brenda has a courage that inspires me. She isn't ashamed. She isn't afraid of all the ways people will judge and criticize her for her honest telling of her story.

She is safe and secure and bold in the love of her God. Because of that, I know her story is going to bring freedom and life to many.

Joshua Harris

AUTHOR'S NOTE

In writing this book I have relied primarily on my memory and, when able, the recollections of friends in the stories. The story is as fallible as any human memory. I have done my best to remember rightly and write accordingly. Most of the names used in the book, but not all, have been changed for the sake of the privacy of those individuals. Sometimes certain details have been omitted or altered to protect anonymity.

ACKNOWLEDGMENTS

In this book, dozens of my family members, friends, and lovers are represented. You were all formative for me.

I'd like to thank my sister Dawny, who taught me to raise my voice, not to shout my opinion but to welcome honesty.

Thank you to my big brother Joey and Uncle Danny for being the first wild men I ever loved; your kind is truly the best.

Kayley and Jamie, you are light beings and I love you.

Mom Mom and Dori, you showed me what activism looks like.

Susie and Erinn: you're dang queens.

Thank you to the magnificent women I call friends, especially Haven, Tara, Tiny, Baillie, Vanessa, Stacey, Lisa, Eva, Courtney, Amanda, Emily and Emily, Tegan, Lou, Tanya, Amy, Jennika, Shosh, Laura, Marissa, Pantea, Io, Ana, Sam, Coco, Yasmin, Tanya, Zoe, Sarah, Mya, Ava, Alexis, Mere, and Kelsey.

I will not be thanking Camille.

To my upstanding lovers, you know who you are. Thank you for being honorable men.

Marco, David, Atlas, Saba, John, Ben, Adam, Anthony, Geej, Kenny, Ramsell, Heyerman, Kutty, Babs, Wyatt, Steven, Mark, Andy, Uncle Pete, and Jimmy Snow—I love you.

Thank you to Langley Fox and Kim Gordon for creating the book cover of my dreams.

To the team at Eerdmans, I owe a debt of gratitude for believing in a challenging book. Anita Eerdmans, you've been a wonderful ally. Thank you for championing stories that expand minds and mend hearts. James Ernest and Trevor Thompson, thank you for your honesty, for your hard work, and for having my back. Thank you to Natalie Kompik for your keen eye and sensible advice. Lydia Hall, you've made this book come to life, and Jenny Hoffman, I'm grateful for your steady hand and unwavering professionalism. Shane White, thank you for heralding the good news of *On Her Knees* to the world.

Finally, to the pastors of my youth, I love you too and hold no animosity.

PROLOGUE

I've been closing my eyes, determining what to write. How could I introduce you to what I've been through these past twenty years? How could I explain that whatever color, creed, sex, sexuality, religion—or lack thereof—you identify with, you might resonate with this book? The reason being, no matter how divided our life experience or ideology, there are universal themes—like fear, shame, and horniness (or the fear and shame that you never get horny)—that help us see one another. Thank God.

I am white, I am blonde, I am middle-class and American. What a cliché. But which one?

Slutty, evil, hateful, whiny, privileged, baby-killing libtard?
Racist, homophobic, prude, ignorant, judgmental, Trump-loving bitch?

Of course, you would never say these things . . . to my face.

Maybe we'd type them at each other on a computer screen. Maybe I'd think these clichés privately of you, and you of me. Or worse, maybe fear and anger will drive us mad enough to shout these slurs at each other, in the light of day. And that, my loves, is a scary prospect. When we assign negative stereotypes to the "other," those opinions become the seeds that blossom into hate.

Or we can lean into love. It is my belief that we are all God's children and that therefore you are no better than me, as I am no better than you. As Martin Luther King Jr. said, "Darkness cannot drive out darkness; only light can do that." When light is shined onto universal human experience—like love, sex, and relationships—we unify, not only with others, but within ourselves. We are meant to be whole.

I cannot promise that I won't offend the conservative Christians and Muslims who believe that my words come at the destruction of God's. I cannot promise Gen Z that I will represent perfectly everything you've been teaching me, from gender to race to sexuality. I myself am wildly imperfect, as you are about to see.

My YouTube channel is called God is Grey because, though divinity resides in absolute truth and perfection—in black and white—we are stuck here on earth, contending with the grey. Grey areas and our dealings with them can make us judge one another, and ourselves most of all. The honest exploration of these grey areas, however, holds the key to unity and to our healing.

On Her Knees is a mess, full of human mishaps. I ask for your grace as I give you mine. Love is the greatest commandment there is, after all.

With love,
Brenda

INTRODUCTION

There's this terrible story in *I Kissed Dating Goodbye* by Joshua Harris. He wrote the inverse of a happily ever after, and I'll never forget it. This story, the supposed retelling of a girl's bad dream, became a nightmare for millions of Christians.

> It was finally here—Anna's wedding day.... Anna walked down the aisle toward David. Joy surged within her. This was the moment for which she'd waited so long.

It was true: Christian girls were waiting to be wed. Really, we were waiting to have sex.

At least, we were supposed to be waiting to have sex.

Despite being outwardly nonreligious, my mom and dad were tight-lipped about intercourse. It took a while for them to admit they were a pair of divorcées on their second marriage. My brother Kris sat, mouth agape, at our Polish Christmas Eve: "I'm fourteen and you're just now telling me Mom was married before?" We realized—over a plate of pierogis—that my parents forgot to pass that info on to the youngest of us. They may have been ex-weed smokers coming off the sexual revolution, but their awkwardness on the subject of intimacy would've fooled anyone. Our Catholic-guilt-infused household was one where bodies tensed at the sound of a moan on late night television. If I sat in front of the TV, parents directly behind me, I'd cease to breathe while Elizabeth Perkins offered her breasts to Tom Hanks in *Big* or when Patrick Swayze wrapped his arms around Demi Moore at the potter's wheel in *Ghost*. Entering puberty in a sex-silent household, the topic became humiliating and intriguing in equal measure. I needed to know more.

Thankfully—or so I'd thought—my hip, young, kinda hot youth pastor talked about sex often. Pastor Scott gifted me a black and gold NIV Bible with "Brenda Marie Davies" embossed on the leather. The inside read, "Pfeiff, Every answer you'll ever need is within these pages. Always, P. Scott." "Always?" An electric surge knocked my knees. Amen and Hallelujah!

Pastor Scott called me Pfeiff like Michelle Pfeiffer. And you might cry "Perv!" but he was the only person who made me feel pretty in my metal braces and with a constellation of acne strewn across my forehead. I never had a negative experience with Pastor Scott, anyway. He was earnest and kind. He read us Jeremiah 29:11: "'For I know the plans I have for you,' declares the Lord, 'plans to give you hope and a future.'" He said this ancient verse was penned for evangelical teens. Standing on the teal carpet of a reclaimed strip mall shop, at youth group, our Jesus-lovin' futures were bright. I worshiped the Lord in Cherry Hill, New Jersey, and the Master of the universe was talking to me.

I cherish certain experiences from this time period. Pastors Scott, Matt, Tanya, and Mike presented the Bible in a way that was accessible and inviting. In contrast to the stoic hymns of Catholicism, the cool Christian teens were bumping Jars of Clay and DC Talk. In youth group, I prayed aloud like a powerful woman of God. I was hot like Michelle Pfeiffer. My life meant something, and it would mean something even more when I got older. "Just you wait," I'd think while Brooke and Mandy teased me for having a coughing spell in pre-algebra. "He knows the plans He has for me." I survived the cruelty of public high school by repeating this verse and praying in the company of sexy babes like John Adair.

John Adair had bright green eyes. He had to be kind to me because he was a Christian.

"Hi, John." My intestines tangled at the sight of him.

"Hey, Pfeiff."

I'd do anything to graze his sun-kissed arms. And those thick lips, my God. John Adair's back formed a slim triangle from his shoulders to the top of his hips. I sucked my tongue to calm the sheer emotion of seeing his Adam's apple swell from afar. And, girls called them "lead lines," the indents trailing from a boy's abs down to his . . . *ahem!*

And herein lies the problem.

I'd grown up casually Catholic, but when I attended a born-again "nondenominational" Christian church at twelve years old, my sexual fascination skyrocketed, and with it my anxiety about "saving myself for marriage."

At the periphery of our Message Bibles, we formed a sweaty circle of preteens dying to touch each other, kiss each other, lick each other. We talked about how to avoid premarital sex and how amazing sex would be within our marriages. We talked about sex constantly but not like our secular counterparts. Our sexual desire was innate, inherent, but we called it lust. We called our libidos original sin. If I were to go on a date with and perhaps kiss John Adair, our sinful nature would have gotten the best of us. I'd be a harlot, a Jezebel, or "easy" for making myself desirable and available. John's walk with God required impeccable self-control—including heeding the call to never masturbate. If we "fell" sexually, my female body would have caused my brother "to stumble" (Romans 14:13).

In this fictional scenario with my church crush, our "fall" would not only be a mark against us at the heavenly gates. Our sexual choices would diminish our worth as future spouses. My value, especially as a woman, as a wife, would be in jeopardy. I cannot tell you how many sermons I've heard about my value as a woman.

Most recently, in an e-book titled *You're Worth the Wait*, Christian speaker and author Lisa Bevere writes that "women lose when they give in." In the chic font of a cool, approachable Instagram post, Lisa warns that we women "forfeit our dignity, honor, and strength" when we "give ourselves away too soon. And when you are broken sexually, it makes it incredibly difficult for you to give yourself completely because you are not complete."

Oof.

I don't know about you, but being told the sexually active are "not complete" is like getting a sucker punch to the pussy. It hurts. And if that word offends you, buckle up. This is a Christian book about a Christian girl, but that's not the last time you'll be reading the word *pussy*.

But I digress.

I loved God so much, so profoundly, since I was a kid that when I learned "God cries when you masturbate," the thought itself made me cry. I'd never want to hurt God. You know, the Incarnate God with the genitalia that makes him a man, the God whose literal tear ducts allow him to cry when I masturbate. I was told that sex outside of marriage, even the thought of unwed sex, was grievous to my creator.

Joshua Harris's story, the bad dream, about a girl named Anna, took this fear a step further. *I Kissed Dating Goodbye* required young adults to consider their future spouses when touching ourselves or one another. "The One" was on their way, and they'd be disappointed in our lack of self-control. And Anna's story is worth telling so you'll "understand my heart," as the Christians would say.

Anna is marrying David. Joshua Harris describes their ceremony, attended by family and friends, as "sunlight poured through the stained-glass windows, and the gentle music of a string quartet filled the air."

Anna meets her beau at the altar. While the pastor reads their vows, a woman from the congregation stands up, walks quietly and grabs David's other hand. Another girl stands, then another until "a chain of six girls stood by him as he repeated his vows to Anna." In his dashing tuxedo, every wedding detail otherwise perfect, David is forced to explain the intrusion of these women.

"I'm ... I'm sorry, Anna. ... They're girls from my past. ... I've given a part of my heart to each of them."

Anna's lip quivers. "I thought your heart was mine."

"It is, it is. ... Everything that's left is yours."

In other words, sex diminishes us. People who have sex are less than; they've given something away. That "something" is their inherent value to both God and their future spouse. The nonvirgin was born with a whole heart, but now it's in pieces.

To display this apparent truth in a tangible way, pastors brought Hershey's and Wrigley's to Wednesday night services. The boys were told to break off pieces of chocolate or to chew the sticks of gum and then answer questions like, "Do you like this grody chocolate bar?" "Does anyone wanna chew the gum Anthony had in his mouth?"

"Ew, no!" The boys were repulsed, and rightfully so when it comes to sharing bubble gum. The problem was that the gum was meant to be my body. My sex. These examples were called object exercises, and the revolting thing in each exercise—the gum, the chocolate bar, the clean cup of water the boys spit into one at a time—was meant to symbolize me, a woman.

Never mind the sexually assaulted who didn't have the luxury of "forfeiting their dignity." If you've "messed up" by "causing a brother to stumble," forgiveness is a prayer away. Simply repent and your "sin" will be forgotten by God.

If you expect the "sin" of premarital sex to be forgiven by your future spouse, however, that would be a different story. Human beings aren't always merciful. When I considered both my Creator and "The One," my future husband, I wanted to be above reproach, my heart intact.

My girl group—Kelley, the other Kelly, Maria, and Tara—rushed to the Christian bookstore to pick out purity rings. I settled on a silver band with a heart and a key. It slid onto my wedding finger, and I couldn't wait to wear it to school. I was already kicking up a storm by praying on the front lawn of the high school while yellow

buses whished by and students jeered. My Kent Hovind creation-
ist apologetics exasperated my biology teacher; everyone knew
I was saving myself for marriage, and they laughed. But it was all
good. John 15:18: "If the world hates you, keep in mind that it hated
me first." (Only now do I know that reveling in hatred can be a sign
you're more of an a-hole than a disciple.)

In my doe-eyed ignorance—and I say this with compassion
toward my sweet, young self—I planned a purity ceremony for
my evangelical youth group. My girls and I had the rings. All we
needed was to make our pledge official. One Friday night, while
my peers were somewhere indulging in hard lemonade and indiscriminate hand jobs, we Christian teens were dressed in white,
promising our purity to the Lord. I signed a virginity contract in
the presence of my parents. "If anything happens, that's okay with
us," Mom said. "Our love is unconditional." She was being gentle,
worried that building a sexual ethic on a foundation of shame and
fear would cause it to crumble.

But I was perfect. I was a good girl.

This would be a piece of cake.

"God, send my husband soon. In Jesus's name. Amen."

ACT
1

1

MANSION

The church, as far as I knew, was full of dichotomies. Sinners and saints, good and evil. In evangelicalism, church leaders said these distinctions would be easy to spot.

For example, a barfly is a bit evil or at least not very good. Murderers are terrible unless they've got a testimony. (Abortionists are also murderers, but screw their testimony.) Politicians are crooked, but we'll vote for whoever upholds "family values." It's Adam and Eve, not Adam and Steve. Slutty girls in short skirts need a savior and curse words are a good sign somebody doesn't know the Lord. Virgin = Christian.

Easy peasy. Black and white. Dichotomy.

Of course, moving to Los Angeles, California, at the age of nineteen and navigating the diverse personalities of this city's "fruits and nuts," as Dad calls us, challenges this dichotomous notion. When your body senses she's safer in the presence of Marilyn Manson—the king of shock rock and goth music—than in the office of her youth pastor, these black-and-white methodologies for spotting good and evil soar out the window.

I was stunned, but there I was, new to LA and invited into the presence of celebrity. Manson poured me a cup of German absinthe at the Chateau Marmont. His smeary lips flirted that he'd chop me "into a million little pieces."

Back in Jersey, Pastor Veronica had yelled, "Show them! Show them," until I removed my woolen scarf. She demanded that Mom and Dad see the hickey I'd received from a neck-up make-out session. (For the record, this prompted my mom to rise up from her chair like a raging lioness and tell Veronica to screw herself.)

In both scenarios, let's consider the black and white.

These two people—Veronica and Manson—were acquainted with Jesus. The former prefers her cross turned up, the latter upside down; the former pink cardigans, the latter black leather. But one of these people humiliated me and made me cry, and it wasn't Manson, the "antichrist superstar."

Point being, polarities of good and evil—along with fifty-plus shades of grey in between—show up at the club and the soup kitchen. Life's no Bond movie where the bad guy cries blood, and good girls aren't required to wear pink cardigans. Recognizing who's righteous is much more complex. And if sitting beneath the steeple keeps us no safer than sitting anyplace else, why stop exploring the world?

Besides, I had a convenient Bible text to back me up. Matthew 9:10–13: "While Jesus was having dinner at Matthew's house, many tax collectors and sinners came and ate with him and his disciples. When the Pharisees saw this, they asked his disciples, 'Why does your teacher eat with tax collectors and sinners?' On hearing this, Jesus said, 'It is not the healthy who need a doctor, but the sick. . . . For I have not come to call the righteous, but sinners." And what better place to look for sinners than the Playboy Mansion?

A notable heir had added me and my new best friend Georgie to Playboy's list from the comfort of his Sunset Hill home. This guy was using a black card to cut up cocaine and snort it when we received the confirmation. "Can we really go?" I asked. Georgie and I swung in a transparent egg chair, chain hanging from the ceiling, our legs entangled.

"I don't see why not." Georgie was practically singing. "We're going to Hugh Hefner's!"

By that Independence Day, I'd never had sex. I was abiding by the law by abstaining from alcohol. I loved Jesus, but there I was boarding a shuttle to Hugh Hefner's house.

An intern snapped a photo before stringing a glittery silver band around my wrist. I'd committed to dressing modestly but grew worried the mansion would require more skin. "What's the photo for?" I asked.

"Mmm, I don't know. I think it's to make sure you're hot enough? Like, for the next party?" The staff had popped up a table in the UCLA parking lot and it was crowded with female interns. They looked like the "prettiest girl in high school" from all around the world, and they were commanding the guest list. In the heyday of Paris Hilton and Nicole Richie, these girls streaked their blonde hair black and wore neon leg warmers with pleated miniskirts. I think I was wearing a flannel newsboy cap and white stilettos. Fashion was terrible, but only in retrospect.

I had parked my single-mirrored Civic among the ancient Toyotas and newish Kias. The sad cars of aspiring actors needn't clog the streets of Bel Air. So Hef, as he preferred to be called, transported his curated strangers from a UCLA parking structure to his estate.

Teetering on heels, I climbed in the shuttle. It was the Fourth of July, and everyone was donning red, white, and blue. A sultry redhead sucked a Bomb Pop and waved for Georgie and me to sit beside her. "First time at Hef's?"

"Is it that obvious?" I was a confident girl, but this bikini-clad Jessica Rabbit sniffed out my insecurity. I wasn't anxious about meeting new people; I loved meeting new people. I was worried that God—the master of the universe—would be mad at me. Matthew 9:10 was at the forefront of my mind, but had I taken God's Word too far? After all, I intended to have fun. Was it against the rules to enjoy your time with sinners? I feared so. Georgie clamped my thigh with her paint-stained fingers. "What's wrong?"

"Nothing." I couldn't explain this church-given anxiety to Georgie. She was an emancipated girl with a sexy French boyfriend and a brigade of hip LA friends. She licked an index finger and smeared saliva across my cheek. I flinched at the sensation. "Oh no. Am I a mess?"

Swapping spit grossed me out, but Georgie's attention was like a warm spotlight. She could dress me up, spin me around, and make me electric slide for all I cared. She'd strung fake daisies through my hair and wing-tipped our eyes for the party. "You had a little smudge. You look perfect, Bren."

I'd moved to LA clueless, but Georgie was building me up as a woman. I wanted to be an actress, but I didn't know how to get an agent. This Eastside goddess was teaching me the nuanced rules of the LA game, from Silver Lake's Happy Foot Sad Foot sign to the waves of Venice Beach. She was the dame of fashion, art, and of course partying. People loved to be in her presence, to be seen; and I wanted her to see me too.

Georgie said it was one of her all-time dreams to see the iconic mansion. Our attendance predated the reality show *The Girls Next Door*, so the estate was shrouded in mystery. I'd heard about movie stars on drugs and orgies in the grotto. The place was extraordinarily "sinful."

My gut clenched as the "Bunnies at Play" signs sharpened into view. They were staked into the grass and were the only thing worth noticing until—behold—the Slip-'N-Slide. Buxom beauties plopped their butts at the tippy-top and careened down the hill into a shallow pool of water. Giggles trickled through the shuttle windows and . . . never ever has a girl been more terrified of a pool party. I was paralyzed by fear.

And this is what you have to understand about Christianity. The message is: Be good. Be very, very good. Live above reproach. Pastor Matt said, "Imagine you're doing something you shouldn't be doing. And now, imagine that Jesus walks through the door while you're doing it."

Hearts stop.

After all, most of us were imagining masturbating, or yelling at our mom, or dinging the neighbor's car and not saying anything. And then, "Oops! Hi, Jesus!"

In those teaching moments (and there were more than one), youth group kids made a silent contract between our Creator and our impressionable little souls: We wouldn't do anything Jesus didn't like. At least we'd try.

Mind you, the list of things they told us Jesus didn't like were total BS. I mean things Jesus literally never once talked about in his life, like gay sex, smoking weed, overeating, or loud girls. Pastor Matt, Pastor Phil, and every pastor in between told me Jesus hated these things. Or Jesus was delivering this message on behalf of his Father, who really, really hated these things.

To the god of my Christian youth, the god of tear ducts and male genitalia, sexuality was the single most offensive form of sin. And gay sex? Don't get me started on gay sex! Despite all the inner turmoil I received from church, I never had to suffer like the gays. My unmarried sex would be sinful, but la-di-da, it happens. I mean, the "la-di-da" came with tears, repentance, and an unyielding sense of eternal doom, but at least I wasn't an abomination.

Still, while the Playboy shuttle drove up to the Playboy Mansion—a landmark of hedonism—I began to unravel. Georgie pinched my thigh again. "Babe? You ready?"

"Yes."

Through the iconic double doors, into the marble foyer, a Lurch-looking guy presented a tray of champagne. Georgie grabbed a glass. "Don't mind if I do." A painting of Hef in his silk robe hung at the crescendo of a double staircase. We made our way to the backyard.

People were smiling ear to ear, clinking glasses and embracing to say hello. Cotton candy swirled into pink and blue fluff while guests drizzled butter on freshly popped corn from the circus popcorn machines. We passed a buffet of crab legs, chicken skewers, broccolini. And I'd later learn that no matter what the party, Hef always had sushi.

Georgie popped a few tuna rolls into her mouth. "God, look at this pool!" Bunnies splashed beneath the warm sun, and a waterfall cascaded into the pool. I watched Georgie frolic and wished I could be happy too. I had to remain vigilant. There was darkness in this place, and I couldn't allow it to suck me in.

Georgie's eyes grew wide as saucers. "Let's go to the grotto!" Oh God, I thought. I didn't want to see people having sex. I was already playing with fire, and Jesus would have my head for doing anything worse. "Was partying at the Mansion really worth it?" he'd say before banishing me to the flames of hell. The way to avoid damnation would be to reflect Him. I'd be the good girl every pastor told me to be. I wouldn't drink, smoke, or flirt; and I'd only look at the orgy for one millisecond. I couldn't risk Jesus walking in and asking me what on earth I was doing there.

By the time my mind ran through the Nine Circles of Hell, Georgie and I had found the infamous grotto. I braced myself for legs in the air and asses pounding a bevy of beauties but found—alas!—a couple in calm conversation. They regarded us with a quick smile before returning their attention to each other.

Georgie deflated. "Let's keep exploring."

I hadn't realized how tense I'd been until I allowed myself to breathe again. The worst of it was over; the grotto was supposed to the epicenter of sin at the mansion. But I couldn't shake the fear that God would be mad at me.

I wrung my hands while Georgie and I made our way through the bathrooms. A cavernous hall led to several doors, each a stone-walled washroom. We passed a few giggly girls with red, white, and blue body paint for bikinis. Costume jewels outlined what would have been their thongs and underwear. Each girl's hair was curled, teased, and sprayed to high heaven. Georgie dragged me through the nearest door; her jaw dropped. "Isn't this unreal?" She pulled her panties to her ankles and plopped on the toilet. "I mean,

I've gotta learn to body paint like that for Burning Man. It's amazing." Georgie would wind up body painting her breasts for Burning Man. And I would get so fed up with the trappings of modesty that I'd volunteer to be nude and body painted for a Pharrell music video. But, of course, I didn't know any of that yet. Instead I was investigating toiletries to distract myself from eternal damnation. I fingered through a basket of wet wipes, tampons, Q-tips, and—gasp!—condoms. The flagrant suggestion that sex was permitted in this bathroom tipped me over the edge. My heart kicked up a beat, and I struggled to breathe.

It's okay, I thought. I'll never come back here again. Please forgive me, Lord. If it helps, I can be more blatant about not drinking. I'll make a show of my, "No thank you," next time Lurch comes around with the champagne. Maybe then people will notice that I'm different and we can kick up a conversation about Jesus?

And before we continue, it's worth noting that the anxiety I experienced was deep-seated and real. Fear of hell is inhibiting if not downright paralyzing. And my belief that God would hate me for seeing condoms in a bathroom stemmed from years of indoctrination. This assumption had nothing to do with how I sensed God in moments of prayer and reflection. But the church taught me my "feelings" were invalid. Jeremiah 17:9: "The heart is deceitful above all things." I was forced to navigate right and wrong through a black-and-white lens. And to assess sin in the real world, my tools for recognition were arbitrary. (Like, Manson wears lipstick = bad; Pastor Veronica never curses = good.) Of course, anything sexual outside of marriage is bad. Therefore, condoms in a bathroom are cause for concern.

At the Mansion, an internal hell was hurting me, while Hef and the bunnies never did me any harm. However, the array of personalities in any place does have the power to hurt people. A business founded on the exploitation of women's bodies is often a dangerous place for the vulnerable. Holly Madison later claimed that her relationship with Hef was a nightmare. She shared her eighty-some-year-old boyfriend with two other women. They simulated orgies for him in scheduled shifts. I'll give credit to Hef for prompting Americans to talk about sex and for skirting the norm and putting Darine Stern—a black woman—on Playboy's cover in the '50s. But it's hard to imagine that being one third of Hef's harem creates a healthy sexual dynamic between you and him. Especially when the guy has a painting of his own face leading into the master bedroom.

My own experience, however, was positive. I thought God hated my being at the mansion, but someone was about to prove me wrong. God wasn't mad at me. As a matter of fact, I was in the right place at the right time.

When Georgie and I left the bathroom, we crashed into an older woman smoking a slim cigarette. Her brow raised at the sight of us. "Hello, ladies." She pulled a strand of my hair and pointed to the fake daisies. "Very groovy. You're from the wrong era, no?" The woman said. "Could I introduce you to my daughter?"

It was an abrupt ask, but Georgie and I were up for anything. This woman turned out to be a porn star from the '70s, her one-piece bathing suit accented by a metallic knit shawl. She was calm and seasoned. She said her daughter couldn't relate to the overly excited, surgically enhanced bunnies of the Mansion. At least, her daughter didn't want to relate.

As Georgie and I trailed behind the porn star, I was relieved to have a purpose and direction. Meeting someone new might ease the shame.

We approached the table and spotted a solitary girl. She wore oversized shades and a big straw hat. She ashed her cigarette into a glass. "What?" The girl was preemptively annoyed by the sight of her mother.

"I've got some girls here. I think you'll like them."

It was strange but—in retrospect—no different than any mom helping any daughter play nice at a pool party.

The girl grinned. "Thanks, Mom." She playfully shooed her away. "Sit down if you want."

Georgie was game to be kind. She and I both loved a challenge, a tough nut to crack. This girl was unapproachable and cold. Georgie aimed to warm her up. "Your mom's a trip. She said you hate it here? You're crazy. I love it."

It was then that the girl removed her shades.

My heart stopped.

She was a successful actress—for the sake of her privacy we'll call her Bella Oakland. But I wasn't starstruck. This was different.

Bella and Georgie got to talking, and I excused myself to make a call.

I found a reclining chair by the pool, sat back and pulled out my Instagram-less, mapless Nokia phone. I dialed my mom, and she picked up on the second ring. "Hi!"

"Mom, I was so nervous to tell you where I am. But now I know I'm supposed to be here. Don't be freaked out."

Nowadays Mom is used to her daughter's frantic calls, but back in the day I was three thousand miles from home and could boast about three friends whom I barely knew. I needed Mom, and she knew it. "Okay, what?"

"Go up to my bedroom and look at the mirror. There's a yellow sticky note on there. Tell me what it says."

I heard her feet pad up the carpeted stairs and into my childhood bedroom. "Okay, what am I looking at?"

"On the mirror. There's a yellow sticky note. What does it say?"

"Bella Oakland."

I smiled. Resting on the lounge, I could see topless girls jumping on Hef's trampoline. The man himself wore a sailor's hat and was nursing a cocktail in the distance. "Mom, I don't know why I'm here, but God wants me to be here. I'm at the Playboy Mansion."

"Okay."

"I'm not obsessed with Bella Oakland or anything. She just popped in my head one night while I was praying. I wrote her name on a sticky note to remind me to pray for her at night. And I did pray for her. I've been praying for her for years."

Mom was stunned. "Wow, Bren." God shot a message to my younger self, and it only made sense now, in this very moment.

"Please don't be mad. I'm supposed to be here, right? That's the proof. Just like Jesus would've been. Hanging out with sinners."

"Yes, he would."

My heart was at peace. God gave me Bella's name because He knew one day I'd be at the Playboy Mansion, agonizing that I shouldn't be. And whether or not you believe I'm a lunatic for saying so, it doesn't matter. What matters is that meeting Bella Oakland after writing her name on a sticky note made me second-guess everything I'd been taught. Pastors told me that Hollywood would be dangerous and evil, that its people's influence would drag me to hell. But I was sitting in the hub of hedonism, in the presence of the king of smut himself, and I sensed no danger. No one was pressuring me to do drugs or to bang them for a movie role. This barbecue had the same polarities of light and darkness as a church picnic. Depending on the partygoer, I sensed happiness, desperation, loneliness, or joy—the same emotions I felt radiating off people at church.

The truth is, we can't tell that a person is righteous based on the temporal evidence, like their location or attire. You have to look a person in the eye. You have to check in with your body, your animal instincts, and assess whether a person's safe. In this case I was wrong to assume others were "sinners" based on where they spent their Fourth of July.

That yellow sticky note focused my purpose into exceptional clarity. I'd been a fearful girl, unsure of her every move. That sticky note reminded me that I knew what I was doing. I came to LA to love. I came to LA to deepen my wisdom and to elevate my soul. That sticky note was God telling me, "Brenda, you got this. Keep going."

2

STEEPLE

The freedom I'd experienced at the Mansion was in stark contrast to the vibe of my apartment, which I shared with two Christian girls. I crept through the door after midnight, wishing I could share my Bella Oakland experience. I wanted to tell my roommates, Jess and Michelle, that God's bigger than we thought. I wanted them to know I was at the Playboy Mansion but that God wasn't mad at me.

I feared I shouldn't say a thing.

Moving to LA at nineteen, the way I knew to connect with people was through church. Church would be a community of like-minded people who worshiped God on Sundays (and Tuesdays and Wednesdays and more). In many ways, church was safe because I knew the answer to everything. As a matter of fact, knowing everything is quite a problem for evangelicals. Nowadays I abide by theologian Pete Enn's concept that the Bible is "ancient, ambiguous, and diverse," an approach to biblical study that frees believers to explore the text with openness and curiosity. I now read the Bible with wonder. But at the time I was in a faith community that said, "the Bible is very clear on homosexuality," or "we know sex before marriage is against God's will." Church leadership claimed absolute clarity on one of the most complex religious texts in human history, one that spans thousands of years, hundreds of authors, and over four hundred English translations. But go ahead, evangelical Brenda. Tell us what you "know" about God.

Michelle was asleep on the couch, a reality show about meter maids buzzing through the TV. I couldn't stand reality shows, but Michelle went from church to her job to watching TV and back again, every single day. I didn't see her do much else.

"Michelle?"

She stirred on the couch. "Hey, Bren."

I dropped my purse on the end table and kicked off the white stilettos. I worried she'd judge my outfit because she was so dang hard on herself.

Michelle worked at our church—let's call it Flowing Waters— and Jess and I both served on the worship team. Whenever someone's job or volunteer position was a public one, meaning they were seen at Sunday services or "on platform," meaning on stage, Flowing Waters required them to sign a contract called the "Standards of Behavior." Michelle was a strict rule follower. Jess and I had a bit more difficulty.

An implied rule at church was that we look happy all the time. Like, hot damn, no matter what's happening in your life you're so fucking happy you could just keel over and die from the bliss. When the worship team commanded we "raise 'em up and praise the Lord," it was our duty to shoot up our hands and shout, "Hallelujah!" This wasn't meant to encourage insincerity (though it did) but to show the present nonbelievers how amazing God is, how happy God makes us. We couldn't imagine a powerful church being a place where people showed their true colors, their perversions or depression. One could lay one's soul bare some other day. Sundays were for outreach.

So we were all really happy all the time. And the contract kicked it up a notch because we also promised to be good. Being "good" in evangelicalism focused on sex, drugs, drinking, and tithing. We gave 10 percent of our income to Flowing Waters and were contractually obliged never to drink to drunkenness, to keep sex within marriage, to abstain from drugs (except with a prescription), and never, ever to be gay or do anything gay.

And if I sound sarcastic and spicy that's because I am. I've worked over a decade to forgive the evangelical personalities who hurt me, but remembering these things still stings. The weight of Flowing Waters' contract was heavy. And after ten years of her diligent volunteering and helping with worship, the entire community would abandon my roommate Jess for being gay. It's hard to process that fact without righteous fury.

But we didn't know this yet. Then, we were three young girls hiding from one another, desperate to fit and fold into Flowing Waters' tight little box. Our pastors told us how to behave and said it was "freedom in Christ."

But at the Mansion, in Georgie's smile, I got a taste of true freedom. As I crept into the room I shared with Jess, I hoped I could tell her what I'd discovered about God that day. We'd have to wait till morning to see.

I wasn't sure Jess would be receptive, but by morning she was leaning on the edge of her bed wanting to hear more. "You got bit by a monkey?"

"Jess, it was so humiliating. Like, only me, right? Bella didn't notice, thank God."

"You just pretended it never happened?"

"Yep. And my finger was bleeding."

Jess laughed. "You need a tetanus shot or something." She stood up to disrobe and hit the shower.

She had this wild mop of curly locks and eyes the size of full moons. Her lashes were long and black and I'd often find them jumping to their deaths from her eyes to her cheeks. "Make a wish," I'd say before she blew another lash into oblivion. Jess was also voluptuous. My curvy friend in high school was hounded by our youth pastors to cover up more and more as she developed. I wondered if Jess had experienced the same humiliation. Either way, she wore loose tees and somewhat baggy jeans. After all, we were all contractually obliged to be modest.

Jess was stepping into the tub but flipped around as if a light-bulb had gone off in her head. "Does Georgie have a Myspace?"

"I think so?"

Jess plopped on my bed. "Lemme see."

"Okay, I'll try to find it." I played it off as if I hadn't been staring at Georgie's Myspace for weeks. The page loaded and there Jess and I were, peering into another world:

Georgie and her friends parading around music festivals in purple lamé bikinis and fringe boots. Click next—Georgie lean-ing over her knees, peach blush dusting her nose. She wore a massive smile and wide rimmed glasses with the lenses popped out. Click next—Georgie and her friends pretending to have an orgy in someone's bathroom. Body parts were blurred to adhere to Tom's guidelines.

Jess gave one of those frowns that said "Damn."

"I know, right? She's wild." And in a moment like this, I was testing the waters. I wouldn't have shown Michelle Georgie's My-space page; but Jess, I wanted her opinion. I thought I detected a longing; it might have been my imagination.

Jess hopped off the bed and headed to the shower. "Well, lemme know when you guys hang out. I'd love to come."

Whoa. Okay. Jess was open. I couldn't wait to introduce her to Georgie.

Back in the hallway I ran into Michelle on her way to the kitchen. She ran past with her head down, seeming to hope that if she moved quickly enough I wouldn't see her. Another real-ity show boomed from the living room, a bunch of rich women yelling and flinging their hands through the air. I sank into the white leather couch with a bag of organic cheese puffs. "What are you watching?"

"*The Real Housewives.*" Michelle made her way back from the refrigerator. She placed a plate of pot stickers on the coffee table and poured duck sauce on top. I wished we could share food, but Michelle initiated a strict shelving system for groceries. She was a rule follower who loved organization. We were different in that way. I was afraid to tell Michelle about Georgie or to ask whether she found Flowing Waters' contract a bit overbearing. But Michelle's desire to ingest hours and hours of garbage television was intriguing. Did she watch others wag their manicured fingers in the air because she couldn't?

Michelle wasn't happy.

Maybe it was me and Jess she found irritating. But I suspected the root of her displeasure was the same as mine: repression of self. It's okay to not sleep around or to not drink, but Flowing Waters' contract was extreme. When we walked into Sunday service, I'd watch Michelle's perpetual frown turn upside down. I'd think, "Is that real?" I myself put on a smile more than I'd care to admit.

Over the buzzing light of our flat screen, I kept this mysterious roommate in my peripheral. I knew we were hiding from one another, in plain sight. I desired sex, adventure, and exploration. I was desperate to avoid all three, but I was quickly tumbling into the latter two. And Michelle, I had no clue what she wanted. She, Jess, and I giggled about our desire to marry ASAP and to vacation here or there, but there had to be more.

We were guilt-ridden over small infractions, we were afraid of hell. Those emotions were paralyzing, but I was beginning to feel my feet again, like that tingle after your limbs have fallen asleep and are waking up. Georgie was waking me up.

3

SINNERS

I'd met Georgie outside the velvet rope of Cinespace. The place was a Tuesday night club on Hollywood Boulevard that boasted the beginnings of the hipster movement. A photographer slithered through the crowd taking party photos while Steve Aoki, Them Jeans, or Ana Calderon manned the DJ booth. Ana managed Steve Aoki's label Dim Mak and, although we're dear friends now, she was intimidating as hell then. Long black hair, all black attire, and I felt victorious if I drew out a hint of her dimpled smile. Ana was kind but selective, of course, because Cinespace became an elite scene.

Kanye would weave through the crowd on a flip phone, passing Katy Perry and Jeremy Scott in deep conversation. There was a stage in the backroom where they'd invite The Presets, Mickey Avalon, and wild babes like Uffie to entertain the crowd. While the Westside girls replicated the 2000s fashion of Paris and Nicole, the Eastside girls of Cinespace flaunted their teeny boobs and fresh tattoos. It was all about fawns, bears, deer antlers and '70s headbands. We'd layer on twenty-seven mismatched items from the Goodwill and hope to appear on thecobrasnake.com.

The "Cobrasnake," as they called him, was the first photographer to upload party photos online the day after a fashion show or event. You'd see him weaving through the crowd wearing thrift-store tees and Tevas with socks. His eyes were bright and searching, shooting the coolest kids with his intrusive flash.

He liked things messy, so you'd roll your eyes into the air or sling your leg over a chair and point to your crotch—anything to get his attention. Other girls didn't even have to try. Cory Kennedy had unkempt hair and let cheese or crumbs or saliva cling to the edges of her mouth, and Mark would snap away with affection. Model and singer C. C. Sheffield also had his attention. Girls seemed to study Cory and C. C. to replicate their vibe and acquire a photo. After all, we didn't have camera phones. Back then, someone had to capture our moments for us.

Georgie and I used to pile in cars and afterparty in the hills. I'd turned twenty-one and started drinking whiskey by then. Jack Daniels helped me ease up and forget about hellfire and damnation, if only for a couple hours. Everyone was dating and hooking up and having sex, and I watched the array of lovers like a kid too small to go on the Tilt-A-Whirl. Everyone knew I was a "good girl," and Georgie would bat bags of cocaine from my reach. "Brenda doesn't do drugs!" She'd shoot me a wink. "Isn't that amazing?" And she meant it. Unlike in high school, my peers didn't tease me for my uppity morality. I was honored and protected for making unusual choices.

But first let's talk about how I met Georgie, the Eastside-of-LA babe.

I'd been stalking her Myspace for weeks. When I clicked the message box, I intended to be bold. Georgie tried to read me the message years later, but I refused to hear it, too embarrassed by my naïveté. It said something like, "Hey Georgie! You are SO beautiful and SO amazing. I live in LA too soooo . . . if you'd ever be down to hang out, lemme know."

Again, this is before social media was "social media." No one knew the rules and speaking to a complete stranger wasn't out of the ordinary. I was looking at a website with pictures, and Georgie was one of the most popular girls on the platform. Her wall gave clues to her whereabouts, her friends telling inside jokes from the night before. "Can you believe Joaquin showed up?! And what he said? ;) hahahaha!" What did he say? I wanted to know more. More importantly, I wanted to be there to hear it myself.

To my utter joy, Georgie wrote back. "Oh, you're so sweet! I go to Cinespace on Tuesdays. Why don't you meet me there?" And then, her phone number.

The butterflies in my tummy fluttered. "Holy, holy, yes!"

Unfortunately, that Tuesday I'd taken the fashionably late thing a bit too far and found Georgie on her way out once I arrived. I'd brought a guy friend from Flowing Waters, and he took a photo of me and Georgie with her digital camera. "I'm so sorry I missed you, Brenda! We'll hang again soon." She crossed her heart in a promise.

The next day I could've fainted when she posted our photo on my wall. "Let's hang for real next time?"

I was afraid I'd never see her again, that I'd blown it, but a week later she invited me and "whoever" to a party at her house. I asked Jess if she wanted to come.

"Absolutely."

Okay, this was good. Jess and I would keep each other accountable in the outside world. Flowing Waters encouraged accountability partners—a.k.a. church friends who would call you out if you were about to sin.

The night of, I was a bundle of nerves. Hours of Myspace research equipped me with a vague sense of current fashion, but I was lost. Jess pulled a headband over her hair. "Like this?"

"Yep. Like they did in the '70's."

I promise we looked ridiculous. I tended to wear jean shorts with textured leggings beneath. For extra money I'd cleaned out the closet of a coworker and plucked vintage dreamcatcher earrings from the Goodwill pile. (I apologize for not being aware of cultural appropriation, by the way. Raised to believe that Christopher Columbus was a hero and that Native American culture was "cool," we white girls passed around Georgie's knockoff Native American headdress and paraded through Silver Lake. I'm sorry, as I believe we all are.)

Back then, there was no Uber. Jess and I cabbed to Georgie's because we agreed to have a drink or two. We were behaving as smartly as we knew how.

When we rolled up to the party, strings of red lights and a wooden kissing booth came into view. Georgie had a Spanish style two story in the heart of hipsterville. You could find your way by making a turn off Sunset at the Happy Foot Sad Foot sign. Jess and I had ventured from the Valley and knew nothing about Silver Lake except that it was cool.

We left the cab and grabbed hands, bracing ourselves for the unexpected. It must've been close to Valentine's Day because the party theme was love. Red, pink, and even pinker construction paper hearts hung from the ceiling. Couples made out in dim corners, and a beautiful, mean-looking girl breezed by before turning around. "You looking for someone?"

"Georgie?"

"In the kitchen." The girl pointed across the dining room before heading upstairs. She wore a slinky red bikini and kitten heels. A sheer '60s style robe grazed her wrists with feathery trim. I found her terrifying. I thought she was amazing.

"Brenda!" Georgie's sweet voice sang from afar.

I perked up and turned to the kitchen. "Hi!"

Georgie slinked over, a bit drunk and pulling her boyfriend by the hand. "You made it!"

"This is my roommate Jess."

Georgie hugged us both. "Have you met David? David, Brenda, Jess."

Hellos all around.

I thought her boyfriend David was beautiful. He was some captivating combination of sheepishness and handsomeness, as though he was embarrassed by his own allure. "Nice to meet you," he said. This was the first time I'd heard a French accent in person.

Georgie didn't yet know I was a "good girl," so she begged us to take topless Polaroids. David slung his arms around her waist and kissed her neck. She paid him no mind, used to his displays of affection. "Everyone has to snap a pic of one boob, or even just the nipple, hang it on the wall, and then we all guess who's who." She handed us the camera and my heart dropped. I was more accustomed to turning down drinks than refusing to take naked photos.

Jess and I sat behind the curtain of the photo booth deliberating. Accountability partners, unite.

"Just one of us could do it. I don't think she'll notice." Jess's eyes were wider than usual.

"We've gotta leave with something. Like, how do we explain it if we don't take a picture?" I intended to give Georgie my Christian spiel, but now was not the time.

Before I could agonize further, Jess pulled her tank top to the side and snapped a pic. We both giggled as she tacked it to the wall. "Well, they're gonna know that's not me." Jess had double Ds.

We emerged from the booth victorious. I'd passed the first test without compromising my standards. Jess had taken a bullet for us both. We clinked our plastic red cups of wine and forged on.

I can imagine myself scrutinizing this party, Georgie observing me. I was kind of awestruck. Innocent, yes, but also intrigued by these artists. I had no sense of fashion or music, and Georgie must've noticed my malleability. *Clueless*, after all, was her favorite movie. I was the Tai Frasier to her Cher Horowitz, and she was dying to give me a makeover. She must've whispered to the Dionne Davenport of this scenario, Sienna (the mean-looking girl in the red bikini), "Brenda is so utterly clueless." Because from this party on, I was Georgie's companion. I was "in."

4

SAINTS

As an evangelical girl, the one thing I could not be was me.

Flowing Waters boasted about our "freedom in Christ" (Galatians 5:1). It told us we were "fearfully and wonderfully made" (Psalm 139:14) and "knit in our mother's womb" (Psalm 139:13) but that we had to "deny ourselves" (Matthew 16:24). These Bible verses were plucked from the ancient text to build us up, but only if what we built "aligned with God's word." Women were to be meek in spirit, training for wifehood but reserving sex appeal for "The One" we would marry, or the one we were married to. Men were meant to practice self-restraint by not touching themselves (Genesis 38:9) and by "leading" their relationships (1 Corinthians 11:3).

And I know certain evangelicals will get their panties in a twist reading this, indignantly countering that God commands us to deny ourselves. But it's worth noting that what we're called to deny is often fundamental to who we are as people. Forcing oneself to fit this paradigm can be painful. One woman described being a Christian female, with innate desires she must deny, as being a lamb baring her neck for slaughter. "That's the posture of a worshiper of God," she said. This sentiment was meant to be uplifting but, damn, doesn't that sound awful? Worse, this sacrifice of inherent self is enforced through out-of-context Bible verses.

I ask, how could God have numbered the hairs on a girl's head (Luke 12:7) and yet hate when she speaks at full volume (1 Peter

3:4)? How could the Creator knit a man in his mother's womb yet be disgusted when he's drawn to penises in lieu of vaginas (Leviticus 18:22)? These contradictions are preached from thousands of pulpits across America. Christians ignore cognitive dissonance in the name of obedience.

The marriage stuff didn't bother me, however. I had the God-given privilege of being pretty dang heterosexual. I also found gender roles a bit sexy. I liked to imagine cooking a warm meal for my future husband before he laid me down and made love to me.

What I did take issue with was everything else.

Women weren't supposed to be leaders, but I found that when I made a bold move a crowd of people would often follow. And I loved the idea of emancipation. The closer I got to Georgie, Sienna, and their friends, the more I envied that they didn't second-guess their every move. Their ethics were intuitive. They were gracious and forgiving because it was the right way to be, not because God would hate them otherwise.

Sienna especially had my attention. She had this fuck-off attitude that I found inspiring. Sienna could be abrupt and cold, but it was because she refused to fake it. Unlike the plastered smiles of Flowing Waters, if Sienna laughed you knew she meant it. And people desired her presence. There wasn't an event where Sienna wasn't front row. There wasn't a Cobra Snake photo album without her picture in it.

Forever generous, she'd buy bottles of champagne at the Chateau Marmont and we'd hold court there for hours. Sienna would clink her flute against mine and call me "Brenzie." Draped in fringe kimonos and art deco jewels, she looked like a silent movie star.

The most intriguing thing about Sienna wasn't her boarding school education or her dad's money. "Spoiled rich girl" was a stigma that pushed her to work hard, attempting to earn what fate had provided her. No, the money wasn't it. I was drawn by her darkness.

At least, I thought it was darkness that Sienna possessed.

Really, Sienna was a freer version of me, sexually fluid and in love with both men and women. She was a sensual babe who moved through the world like a thunderstorm, frightening people. I had this shameful fantasy that I too was unaffected, like her. I'd live off wine and cigarettes. I'd spend evenings between the pages of a book or with a rugged man between my thighs. I'd discard sexual companions and forge on, intact, even while they wept at my doorstep.

Reading this, Sienna might gasp, "I'm nothing like that!" Then she might pause and add, "Well, now that I've given up vodka." Sienna was a terror train on vodka. Hence her newfound affection for tequila. Because, see, Sienna would abandon bad habits for her greater good. She was rational. She assessed issues with the aid of information and research. She cried less, not led by emotion. I wouldn't say she "put her trust in God," but she did believe in redemption.

The religious-minded often make an enemy of intellect, but I was dying to use my brain like Sienna did. And not only Sienna. Many of Georgie's friends were transplants from Paris, like David. Their culture is passionate but nonreligious. I'd been cautioned that LA people were companions of Satan, led by their evil desires and wicked whims. But I couldn't find the weepy, irreparable damage of premarital sex pouring off my new friends. After smoking weed or taking molly, they weren't self-loathing and writhing under God's wrath. I wasn't sure I'd want to try drugs. I knew I'd never be promiscuous. But the freedom of simply not hating yourself and not being scared all the time—that looked amazing.

These thoughts presented themselves like ponies on a carousel until Sienna leaned into me. We were in a booth at Club Bardot, sipping margaritas. "Do you like Davey?" she asked. "He's got a perfect dick."

I blushed. "He's fine."

Sienna smirked and swigged a bit more tequila. "Listen, I know you're a virgin, yes?"

I nodded.

"And you've never been with a woman? You prefer men?"

"Yeah?"

"So, if you're gonna have sex, you should pick Davey." She made a measuring stick of her hands. "*It*'s perfect."

"You mentioned."

This line of questioning didn't bother me. Secular skepticism was an opportunity to share Jesus. My run-in with Bella Oakland was proof I needn't stay beneath the steeple to do outreach. I liked that people knew I was "saving it for marriage."

Sienna and I were playing tic-tac-toe on a napkin when the man in question arrived. "You two going to Marco's?" Davey wore a mauve suit, like he'd been playing trumpet in a swing band. He idolized another time when Frank Sinatra or Elvis Presley might've walked through the door.

Sienna bit her tongue in more ways than one. "We'll be there."

And before Davey left, I saw something I never recognized before. He looked at me as if he were a lion and I were prey. A flash darting through his eyes, his pupils dilating with lust.

I swallowed a wad of spit that had built up in my throat. I had to cough to compose myself.

"You all right?" Sienna whispered.

"Yep."

I'd never been regarded with raw desire. Or maybe I'd never noticed that men looked at me like that. "Saving myself" had become an uphill battle, my hormones raging like Adderall-fueled teens in a metal show mosh pit. And now, with Davey craving my body, I didn't know how I'd contain myself.

❦

"Okay, but you must've done it for a reason." Georgie was drawing hearts beneath her eyes with liquid liner. She looked at me through her vanity mirror, inquiring about the infamous purity ceremony at my old church.

"Let me get this straight." Sienna paced the bedroom, stressed, imagining me signing a virginity pledge. "Your father was there?" Her feet tiptoed between droplets of dried up aquamarine, white, and cerulean paint.

"What were you making, Georgie?"

"Oh! Shoes. I painted the shoes from McQueen's show—"

"Stop!" Sienna put her finger to Georgie's lips. "I'm talking to Brenda."

The girls turned to me. This was the moment to testify. I couldn't deny Jesus now.

"Yes, my dad was there, but no, it wasn't awkward. And I made the choice myself. I heard about purity balls and suggested one to my pastors."

"This was self-imposed?" Georgie asked with care. She and Sienna had softened up and strewn their bodies across the floor, drawing closer with curiosity.

"Well, yeah." And I loved to say, "Jesus resonates. I've been praying since I was a kid and something about his name, especially in the Hebrew, Yeshua; well, yeah, it just resonates." The sentiment was strong but got shaky at the end in presentation. I was worried my new friends would tease me.

But Georgie frowned in approval. "I like that."

"Me too."

The girls were on my side. Not on the side of conservatism or religion or saving sex for marriage, but on my side in general. Whatever I'd shown them, they were beginning to love. They weren't going to allow religion to get in the way of our friendship. The three of us climbed into Georgie's cookie-crumbed bed to watch a movie, as though nothing had changed.

It was disheartening to realize my church was meant to be a

family, that I'd never felt as safe beneath the steeple as I did beneath Georgie's sheets. Her down comforter tickled my nose, and I gazed up at the popcorn ceiling. Georgie twisted my hair around her finger and tugged. "I heard you and Davey have a vibe."

I shot Sienna a playful look of betrayal. "Sure. Maybe. But I'm not gonna do anything about it."

"Well, I think that's wise," Georgie said. "You're twenty-one and you've waited this long. What's the rush?"

Sienna's brows raised with disapproval, but she kept quiet. "More wine?"

"Yes," I said, forfeiting my glass. We drank from pink, rose-adorned goblets, courtesy of the Madonna Inn.

Georgie listened as Sienna's steps faded downstairs and into the kitchen. "Bren, what are you really thinking? You can tell me the truth."

Depending on where and how you were raised, you may think purity culture had no effect on you. But if you recall Britney Spears being slung through the mud for maybe, possibly "losing her virginity" to Justin Timberlake, you'll realize the notion of "purity" is insidious. The church calls out culture for being obsessed with sex, but the church's obsession with not having sex is equally consuming. The "culture"—whether secular or religious—is infatuated by intercourse. As for the Britney rumor, I place "losing her virginity" in quotations because virginity is a social construct. Allow me to explain.

I didn't know that virginity was a social construct when I pledged to "save" it. Virginity was meant to be a gift for my husband. That's what I was told. Nowadays, in the wake of #MeToo, there's an addendum of, "Don't worry. God is righteous to redeem," if a victim's "gift" has been stolen. But the assertion remains: Stay a virgin till marriage. And if you can't, repent.

However, with an objective look at virginity, the definition becomes impossible to nail down. Who's a virgin? A girl who's never been penetrated by a penis? A guy whose penis has never penetrated? In this case, are queer women virgins? How about men who've strictly had anal sex? Do we dignify rape victims with the term, or does a sexual assault null their virginal status?

Frustrated by this notion, some churchgoers broadly claim consensual sexual activity is the loss of virginity. But does this imply a person loses her virginity through a tongue kiss?

And let's dive into that word: *lose*.

"Losing your virginity." What do we lose exactly?

The aforementioned Lisa Bevere insinuates that unwed sex is the loss of our "dignity and strength." Object exercises propose that we lose pieces of our heart, our value. A rose loses its petals, the chocolate bar diminishes to nothing—unless we're married. When you're married, pastors say, sex will be orgasmic and amazing! But that women will eventually dread sex because their spouse wants it all the time. "Men!" female pastors wink and smile. "Am I right, ladies?" Then they'll remind gals at the women's retreat to satisfy their husband's desires (Ephesians 5:22). Christian women are taught that sex is a loss, then a duty.

In evangelical churches across America, pastors promise singles a massive payoff for "waiting" while simultaneously counseling married couples through a myriad of sexual dysfunction.

Linda Kay Klein's book *Pure: Inside the Evangelical Movement That Shamed a Generation of Young Women and How I Broke Free* follows subjects through their journeys with purity culture. The outcome of purity culture is so extreme that experts compare its effects to a combination of post-traumatic stress disorder and complex PTSD. Men have suffered erectile dysfunction, women vaginismus, from decades of systematic shaming around sexual desire. Within purity culture, some victims of sexual assault have been unable to connect romantically, certain they were irreparably damaged. Other women have missed their child-bearing years holding out for God to send "The One." LGBTQ people have suffered abuse and suicidal ideation.

The Bible says, "A good tree cannot bear bad fruit" (Matthew 7:18), and yet churches continue to plant seeds of purity culture, hoping the fruit won't be rotten. (Remind me the definition of insanity again?)

And when the going gets tough, when our notions of "purity" are challenged, we are generally not welcome to express the resulting dissonance in church. This is because the church historically plants its feet in binaries, in the black and white, in the pure and impure, while resisting the complications of nuance. When met with grey areas, we're often told to pray. Without a licensed therapist, without a trauma healing. "Pray."

I'm a huge fan of prayer; I believe in prayer's power. But for what were we meant to pray? To remain unpenetrated until we wed and live happily(ish) ever after?

As for the unhappily abstinent—me, Jess, and Michelle—the rotted fruit of "purity" manifested itself differently.

Unbeknownst to me, Jess was "struggling with same-sex attraction." LGBTQ people in religious communities are often encouraged to adopt this phrase in lieu of calling themselves gay. You could YouTube dozens of sermons in which pastors explain that calling oneself "gay" is to accept deviancy as your identity. The belief—or at least the rhetoric—is that secular LGBTQ people have succumbed to their desires and that those desires are fueled by their choice to identify as queer. "Turn away from the gay lifestyle," they'll say, as though being LGBTQ is a choice.

I once had more compassion for Christians stuck in this mindset. When a religious person warns LGBTQ people of hellfire, it's often because they're terrified of hellfire themselves. (Note the politicians who lobby against gay rights before getting caught having gay sex in their offices.) But today, with biblically sound, LGBTQ-affirming theological resources fully accessible, my patience has waned. Gay people are not an abomination; the way the church treats them is what's abominable. After ten-plus years of tireless, unpaid service, Jess was kicked off the worship team of Flowing Waters. She stopped hearing from our "church family" after she admitted her female roommate was more than a friend.

Michelle, however, remains a mystery to me. She eventually married and had children. But when we lived together, I saw her shamed for having sex before marriage.

Our contract with Flowing Waters forbade us from being alone with someone of the opposite sex, so Michelle sat on the stoop of our apartment building, flirting with her crush, Andrew. Dating at church was about finding "The One," so really they were courting for marriage. Outside, on the stoop, in the dark, they discussed any topic applicable to a happily ever after, including sex.

Andrew was a fellow church kid and a "virgin" in the classic sense of the word. He was tall and cute, one of the more sought-after parishioners in church girls' quest for wedded bliss. I often saw Michelle and Andrew leaning into each other, close enough to kiss, their hands entangled with affection. But on this particular night, Michelle stormed into the apartment, throwing herself against the door and crumbling to the floor. Jess and I ran to her. "Oh, my goodness, what's wrong?" Jess asked.

Between the tears and coughing, Michelle told us. "He—he—he … won't be with a nonvirgin. He can't, he said. He—he—he … can't." Tears trickled down her cheeks, and Jess held her close.

"Why?" I asked, pissed off. I regarded Andrew as judgmental and cruel until I realized, years later, the pain men endure in purity culture. The boys were called to impeccable self-control. They were told that if they waited then the perfect wife would be waiting for them. "The One" would give him the gift of her virginity.

To stereotype, guys can be territorial, like dogs pissing on trees. Historically men have sought to "conquer" women. "Make her mine," they say. To this day, women around the world are subjected to hymen inspections—an inspection that even rapper T. I. requested from his daughter's gynecologist when his daughter was about eighteen, despite the stone-cold fact that an absent hymen is not proof of penile penetration. Point being, even in secular circles, a woman's virginity can be owned by a man, in thought.

Michelle's boyfriend Andrew, like these men taught to conquer, believed his wife would be a virgin. He dumped Michelle after a few days of deliberation.

Jess was hiding, Michelle was ashamed, and me? I was dying of horniness. I'd been masturbating since around five years old. (Please refrain from horror, as this is common. Most of us are inherently sexual, knit together as such in our mother's womb.) That said, promising to abstain from sex at fifteen underestimated how extreme my desire would be at twenty-one. My prayer was, "God, send 'The One' now!"

By then, my sexual history was as follows:

- Dennis was a stoner, a bad boy who pulled fire alarms. I was smitten by his rebellion. I enjoyed being rebel-adjacent. We kissed—with tongue—after I demanded he stop smoking and join me at church. One week later, he'd profess to losing his faith but renewing his devotion to cigarettes.

- In Philly, in the back of Eva's Ford station wagon, I kissed a random boy we met at a party. I agonized the next day, realizing I'd opened a lusty floodgate I didn't have the inclination to shut.

- The hottest guy in acting class, head-over-heels for yours truly, went down on me after a viewing of *The Ring*. I hadn't meant to sleep over, but that movie scared the hell out of me. On the way to school he asked a thousand times if I was okay. He knew I'd broken my promises.

- I touched my first boyfriend's penis. I was amazed that his dick felt like one of those thick, jelly worms you buy at Spencer's Gifts. I thought the movement of his foreskin would hurt, so I hurt him more trying to make it stay in place. Frustrated, he gave me an HJ tutorial so I could get the hang of it, but I was too traumatized to jump back in. We committed to dry-humping from that evening forward.

And that's it—the entirety of my exploits prior to attending Flowing Waters. I'd done a little experimenting, but it felt all right. These experiences weren't increasing my sex drive or ruining my life, which was confusing. I knew I was supposed to feel awful, but I didn't.

If you put this mess of purity culture aside, the story of Christ is one of unconditional love. The Divine sent His begotten Son to experience humanity alongside us, to suffer and die for us. Christ would then reside within, elevating our consciousness and increasing our love for others. With love like that, profound and steadfast, it became more difficult to believe that God would abandon me for these minor sexual offenses.

But only for the minor offenses.

I was conditioned to believe that sex outside of marriage was a grave offense. Although we were told all sin is forgivable, premarital or gay sex seemed completely, utterly, and totally unforgivable. Perhaps it's because sex was presented as the sin in which you fundamentally lost something, like your inherent worth or your chance at a happily ever after.

Or maybe sex felt unforgivable because our pastors said sex, lust, masturbation, and even desire would separate us from God. When you've sensed the Divine since childhood, when you're head-over-heels in love with the Creator, threat of separation is terrifying. We want God on our side, and the evangelical God hates lust. So the choice became clear: To have God, I must forfeit sex; to have sex, I must forfeit God.

5

WOLF

By now I'd spent months with Georgie, Sienna, and the crew. We danced at the hipster spots like Cinespace and Starshoes. Sometimes we'd switch it up for a Hollywood club like Joseph's or Nationalé where promoter Dean May—in his infamous block-letter SEX necklace—would invite us to bypass the line. Britney Spears, Paris, and Lindsay Lohan were often gallivanting inside. Britney would be dancing on a booth, hyping the crowd, and—dang—I couldn't believe the adventure God was sending me on.

I thought of Isaiah 6:8, "Then I heard the voice of the Lord saying, 'Whom shall I send? And who will go for us?' And I [Brenda] said, 'Here am I. Send me!'" I'd go through hell for the Divine. If Jesus needed a girl to save Hollywood, he'd sent me. I was honored. And I wasn't afraid; I was exhilarated. The leaders of "culture," a culture demonized in church as evil, surrounded me now. "Saving the unsaved" was paramount.

Hollywood was supposed to be the den of thieves, a playground for the wicked. Therefore, I wasn't a casual resident of Los Angeles proper: I was an evangelist. Jeremiah 1:4-5: "The word of the Lord came to me, saying, 'Before I formed you in the womb I knew you, before you were born I set you apart; I appointed you as a prophet to the nations.'" Most of us young evangelicals were given this verse, told that God wasn't speaking to the ancient prophet, but to each and every one of us. Armed by this prophecy, I fancied myself a foreign spy in a luxurious trench coat. I'd imagine rolling into a satanic gathering like a divine thunderstorm, bringing the lost back to Jesus. This mission to save others was exhilarating—sexy even—and I knew the most effective way to do it. "I'm a sheep in wolves' clothing." That's how I explained the theory to a skeptical Michelle. She'd begun to notice my absence around the house. Over microwaved pot stickers, under the glare of reality TV, she'd clocked the strange hours of my returns.

"And you have to stay out till 3 a.m. to . . . do what again?"

"To be a sheep in wolves' clothing." Jess unwrapped another candy and popped it into her mouth. "I love that."

Michelle rolled her eyes.

"Okay, so you know how wolves in sheep's clothing prowl around the church, pretending to be good? But they're still just terrible wolves?"

"Yeah."

"Well, I'm like that but in reverse. I prowl around the club like a wolf, but I'm really a sheep."

"Like, she's not getting drunk or stoned or anything, Mich. She's out there, like, shining Jesus. Without being a nerd."

"Yes!" Jess had my back. "I promise, Mich. I'm being good. This is where God wants me to be, out in the world, evangelizing."

Michelle stood to throw her paper plate in the trash. "Okay. Just be careful you don't become a wolf in wolves' clothing."

"She is." Jess sat on her feet like a giddy kid. "Careful, I mean. Not a wolf. It's all so exciting." Nothing was more fun than recounting Hollywood stories with Jess. She worked her ass off at church and couldn't go out with me too often. In theory, I should have denied the classist notion of celebrity, but I got a kick out of seeing stars in the flesh. I loved being around performers because it made me feel that my outlandish dreams were accessible.

I wanted to be an actress, and Jeremiah 29:11—"'For I know the plans I have for you,' declares the Lord, 'plans to prosper you and not to harm you, plans to give you hope and a future'"—had me believing that personal celebrity was an inevitability. I was out to save Hollywood. And I don't know whether church amplifying a teen's importance was good or bad, but I lean toward good. Because, dang, why not tell kids to chase their dreams? Reach for the stars and you'll still catch a cloud, la, la, la.

Although my larger mission—to evangelize—was set firmly in place, I fought to suppress the screaming of my hormones. I mean, I don't know if that's technically true, that hormones are what drives one insane. But I do know that the urge to have sex became more of a hunger cue than a desire.

My body's suggestion to pursue sex grew from an irritating whisper to the sound of nails screeching down a chalkboard. And there were cute boys everywhere. Babes watched movies at the Egyptian Theatre; they perused Carnival Books and tried on pirate patches at Ozzy Dots. I saw at least a dozen boys a day I'd love to kiss, to touch, to—

"Chill," I'd say aloud. "Calm down." The invitation to commit a grave sin—the sin of unwed sexuality—was everywhere I looked.

Back at home, in the Valley, I'd allow Bible verses to wash over me like an ice-cold shower. I prayed for God to diminish my sexual desire or to bring my husband—"Quickly!" I'd ask for mercy, for God to reveal a timeline of when he intended to send "The One." I was furious that I was young and that my boobs perked heavenward but that no one could enjoy my body. "When is he coming?" I begged.

Years later, I realized that sex had been a closed door between God and me. It was the only thing for which I'd scream requests to the sky without hearing an answer. Therefore, I didn't ask the right questions. Like, "God, am I allowed to fall in love and have sex without a wedding dress?" Or, "God, is my flesh as evil and disgusting as they say?"

I believed God was the author of volcanos and thermodynamics and euphoria and whatever zaps you between the thighs when somebody wants you. But I had to wait for marriage, and there was no one I wanted to marry.

I was enjoying my blossoming LA friendships. I wished to put off marriage, to explore the wild personalities of the city. But, without a "till death do us part," my mind kept spinning

I wanted to please God, but I didn't know how much longer I could wait.

Breaking into Hollywood, meanwhile, was turning out to be as hard as they say. I took jobs as a personal assistant, a closet organizer, a bottle service girl—anything to pay the bills. Georgie and Emily launched a clothing line—let's call it Pretty Pony—and when they paid me to model I considered it all in good fun. When I received a call from Next Models, offering me a modeling contract, I was stunned. From my point of view, I was a girl playing dress up with my best friends, occasionally tricking other brands into hiring me. It's a dang shame I saw it that way too. I might've taken my career further had I stopped fancying myself an intruder.

This lack of confidence could be traced back to my introduction to the fashion world. When I was seventeen, Mom brought me—at my request—to Philly for a cold call, which meant I wasn't referred. While we waited to be seen, a model booker walked by and pushed her nail into my forehead. "A zit." She frowned. "Cover up."

In the casting room, the bookers asked me to walk. They deemed me "a bit large." Actually, "twenty pounds overweight." Granted, I was an indiscriminate eater, believing a bagel plus a Snickers bar to be a well-rounded breakfast. But after the casting, "a bit large" ran through my head so often that I suffered a bout of anorexia. My eating disorder worsened over time, first compelling me to abstain from lunch and then dinner. At the height of my disease, I ate cereal with water for breakfast. For dinner, I'd allow myself an apple, and I would be so hungry that I ate the core. I lived like this for a year and a half.

I wish I could say I know how to beat anorexia so I could help others. But, truth be told, I was anorexic and then, one morning, I was not. My prayer had been that God would free me from my eating disorder and, to this day, I believe that He did.

More often than not, however, our prayers must accompany real-life action and the hard work of healing. Not every prayer is answered so quickly or concisely. I begged for my husband daily—hourly even—and God didn't seem to come through.

With anorexia, my body wept for food, shrank in size, grew fuzzy peach fur on my skin to protect me from the cold. My body shouted loudly that I was hurting her with starvation, but I continued to deny her needs. And I must admit, starving for sex became as consuming as starving for food.

Sex is not essential like food, but our survival does depend on both. Sexlessness won't kill the individual, but sexlessness would kill off our entire species. And in that way sex is both essential and not.

Fear-based sexual repression can do some perverse things to the brain, too. While abstaining, my hormonal, physical desire for sex devolved into an obsession. For this reason, I've called repression the devil. If you believe that concept to be hyperbole, allow me to explain.

Purity culture stunted and warped my prepubescent sexual development, like a tree growing through cement. My sexuality became a sin before I had a handle on its power. Masturbation—even that—was the first thing I was told would offend God. Song of Solomon 8:4: "Daughters of Jerusalem, I charge you: Do not arouse or awaken love until it so desires." Youth pastors plucked this line of poetry from the explicit, erotic novel that is Song of Solomon to convince kids not to masturbate. How's that for irony?

You've got an out-of-context verse from Song of Solomon and the root of Onanism, Genesis 38:9, which says, "But Onan knew that the child would not be his; so, whenever he slept with his brother's wife, he spilled his semen on the ground to keep from providing offspring for his brother." This ancient verse torments modern men into not touching themselves. God was allegedly infuriated by Onan's spill.

If you're not satisfied with these two irrelevant Bible verses used to address masturbation, (1) neither am I, and (2) allow me to present the verse that suppresses and perverts the modern believer's sexual desire *for real*. Matthew 5:28 says, "But I tell you that anyone who looks at a woman lustfully has already committed adultery with her in his heart." That's right. God's coming for your thoughts, ho, and he's not going to like them!

This evangelical thought-policing morphs into self-policing, to the extreme. The demand to be "pure in thought" plants an adolescent shame so deep and fundamental that a full-grown adult may not have the tenacity to climb their way out into sexual health.

The more frustrated I became with abstinence, the more perverse became my "devilish" thoughts. I wrote in a journal that I knew abstinence was wrong and that I'd never wish it upon anybody, but "What if someone took it away? It would be gone, and I could be normal." From there, ravishment fantasies became the norm when I touched myself.

After a couple decades of waiting, there was no need to rush to a decision. I did make an earnest choice to abstain, even if I'd lost sight of the reason. I decided to call a friend.

"Lindsay?" Lindsay was someone I'd grown to trust at Flowing Waters, a married friend of mine.

"Brennie!"

Petite and bubbly, Lindsay would cruise in and out of church with her miserable-looking husband on her arm. I don't know what his deal was, but the guy wasn't afraid to wear resentment on his sleeve. They were young, they were Christian, they were married for life.

"Sorry to call you so late."

"Aw, girl, you know I don't mind!" Linds has a Southern twang I adore.

Spinning a phone cord around my fingers, I had to ask what she thought of sex. Did she wait for marriage? Was she bummed or overjoyed? "Tell me everything."

She laughed and sighed. "Aw, girl. Well, you know, it's life. I had sex before marriage, and I do regret it."

"Why?"

Lindsay wasn't sure, but she theorized that had she been "pure" her marriage would be better. By the time we'd hung up I shrugged. My sexual desire had reached a fever pitch. Asking me to imagine a regrettable day in the distant future when my "One" would be (maybe) mad at me wasn't enough. Worst of all, I asked a few more couples, and they recounted similar stories. Like, "I didn't wait—but, dang, I wish I had."

What a revelation! No one had waited. No one that I could find at Flowing Waters. I was like a lone, virginal ship, out in the "pure" sea all by myself. And did this knowledge make abstinence more painful? Oh yeah. These personal stories wouldn't suffice.

But I was devoted to my faith. I still am. If I were to throw in the towel on my virginity one sunny afternoon, I'd need to know why. Conversely, if I determined I had to wait, I needed that "why" too. I refused to drift into sin, and I couldn't play dumb with the Master of the universe. I'd have to press into biblical research.

Now, let's be honest. My research didn't go that deep. Your girl wasn't scouring the ancient Hebrew and Greek, poring over the nuances of biblical translation. None of that. I opened my old NIV, the one in which Pastor Scott scribbled "Pfeiff," and read all the passages alluding to sex. What I found was confusing.

There were passages in the New Testament on sex, but I struggled to grasp their meaning. At a cursory glance, the Bible speaks of "sexual immorality," but in broad terms. It seemed my youth pastors were the ones hellbent on making God's rules more specific. The worst offender for perverting God's word into a long sexual innuendo was the True Love Waits Bible. Each page presented a fresh reason to preserve your purity. And our churches themselves made a list—not explicitly stated but heavily implied. Sexual activity was forced into the binary of "pure" and perverse. If something wasn't explicitly stated by our pastor, we parishioners would guess. See the next page for the Evangelical Sex Rules, as I understood them.

Yet, the Jesus of the Gospels harps on love and respect. Of course, there's no mention of booty calls or sexting. Jesus appears more concerned with loving others as ourselves. He cautions us to be wary of excess, to remain vigilant and good despite acquired wealth. He's also concerned with justice and with outcasts and lepers. Jesus lays his hands on the sick and filthy, refusing to withdraw his compassion. He says the least are the greatest and that children know best. And as a child (if you'll allow me to consider twenty-two young), my earnest view was that Jesus didn't require my virginity. He upheld marriage, yes. But what of pre-marriage? Jesus didn't offer a guide. When it came to premarital sex, Jesus is King, and I saw no indication that he'd love me any less.

Still, I wasn't satisfied. I'd waited this long, and Jesus's grace wasn't a decent excuse to mess things up. I had to look deeper, and it was in the midst of this seeking that I had a pivotal conversation, one that would change my life.

THE EVANGELICAL
SEX RULES

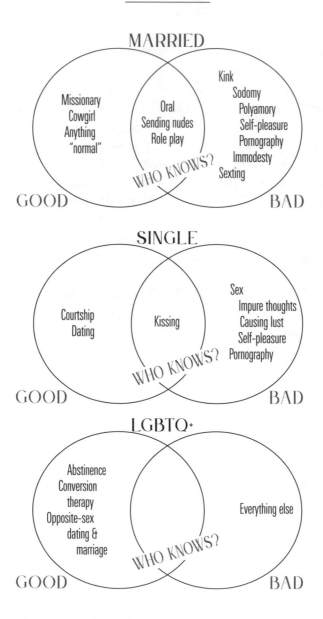

MARRIED

Missionary
Cowgirl
Anything
"normal"

Oral
Sending nudes
Role play

Kink
Sodomy
Polyamory
Self-pleasure
Pornography
Immodesty
Sexting

WHO KNOWS?

GOOD   BAD

SINGLE

Courtship
Dating

Kissing

Sex
Impure thoughts
Causing lust
Self-pleasure
Pornography

WHO KNOWS?

GOOD   BAD

LGBTQ+

Abstinence
Conversion
therapy
Opposite-sex
dating &
marriage

Everything else

WHO KNOWS?

GOOD   BAD

I met Brandon in a recording studio. He had hair past his shoulders, tendrils of silk curling in seven shades of brown. His eyes were kind, with spider legs for lashes. He had a strong jaw and a battered leather jacket, the emblem of his Orange County skate crew sewn on the back.

At first I hadn't been stunned by Brandon. He was kind and attentive and he liked me—all traits that I liked. But I was sick with anxiety. The script of horniness and hunger played through my head like a record on repeat. Not to mention, dating a non-Christian seemed pointless. I could only inspire a monk-like patience in my partners for a few months, or until they realized I was serious about waiting.

With Brandon I figured we could make out until the big V card announcement. I intended to wait, and I doubted that Brandon—with his leather jacket and slashed tees—would be open to my piety.

Still, I anticipated us making out. He was a babe, and I hadn't kissed anyone since college. There was privilege in not making love, the lack of physical intimacy making it easier to be rejected for not "giving it up." Which, by the way, is a phrase I now find infuriating. What do we "give up" exactly? Sex is an experience to be shared, not an unarmed robbery.

For our second date, I sat across from my future husband—over burnt black coffees—and he convinced me, beyond a shadow of a doubt, that it was time to have sex.

The place was in the Valley, subpar, with drinks that tasted like you'd bought them at a truck stop en route to Arizona.

Brandon and I traded the usual stories. In our fresh early twenties, there wasn't much to share. He's an only child; I grew up with three siblings. We were raised on opposite coasts, my upbringing with proper seasons and his without. Brandon loved skateboarding. I admitted I hadn't tried and it freaked me out. "You wouldn't fall," he said. "I'd catch you." We liked music and art, we loved Myspace and seeing live shows. He wasn't familiar with the hipster scene, keeping his head down and devoting time to work—unlike myself, who went out every night. Splitting the rent of a small room and modeling once a week made my life easy-breezy. "They're gonna take me on tour this summer," he said. "Europe and everything." He tucked his curls behind his ears, and I thought, "He's cute." He really is. I could imagine kissing him. And then he dropped the bomb.

"Wanna hear the craziest shit?"

Of course I did. "Of course I do."

"Okay, so you know our drummer?"

I remembered the guy, hair buzzed to his skull, liner smeared across his eyes. He was emo, taking down-angle pictures for Myspace (weren't we all?). He pretended to have a chip on his shoulder, but I suspected a lack of confidence to be his plight.

"You know, he's always writing songs about girls breaking his heart, blah, blah, blah. Ivan, our lead singer, you know, takes them. They're good. But the guy's never fucked."

A wad of spit appeared in my throat. "What?"

"He's never had sex. He grew up super Christian. He promised God he would only have sex with his wife or some shit."

"And?" I was relieved I hadn't told him I was a virgin. If he thought his bandmate was a freak, then I'd be a freak too. Brandon found the situation laughable, the "situation" being chastity.

He must've read the horror on my face. "I'm not making fun of his sexual choices—just so you know. All power to him."

I smiled.

"It's just . . . well, that was his deal. Virgin until marriage. Right?"

"And?"

Brandon gripped his hands on the table, as though without an anchor, this story would drift him away. "And! And?" He laughed. "He brings this random girl home last night—a blonde with fake boobs—comes out in the morning, while we're all eating fucking cereal, and he's like, 'I had sex.'"

50

Everything stopped.

I didn't perceive myself at a table, with a coffee, talking to a soul. I was alone, in a clear, white room and to the ether I said, "I'm gonna have sex with this guy." My voice echoed back, "I'm gonna have sex, sex, sex, sex . . ."

When I returned to earth, Brandon came back into view.

I bought time with a "What?" allowing him to reiterate the story while I considered this new reality—this reality where my purity pledge would be ripped in two. Soon I'd line up with the other losers who couldn't wait for sex another day. I'd tell my One, "I'm sorry. I regret it." But there was no choice. Sex with this guy was inevitable. I'd been begging God for an answer for months. I was like that guy in the story about a flood. Where he won't leave home because he trusts God to save him. But then the whole town floods and he winds up on the roof. And a canoe goes by, offering life, but he says no, he's waiting for God to save him. And then a helicopter swings by and drops down a ladder, and again he refuses, insisting that God's gonna save him. And you know what? That guy died.

I hoped to recognize my savior. I'd scoured Flowing Waters for virgins; I'd asked the Bible to illuminate a few. I didn't know a virgin over twenty-one years old. The drummer—the truth that he'd thrown his virginity away—was my helicopter, tossing a rope to my lone, virginal ship.

"Let's go to your place."

I'd interrupted Brandon midsentence, which would have been rude had it not been good news. He leapt from his chair. "Sure. Of course."

Back in his Valley apartment, one he shared with five guys, I asked him to grab a condom before we'd kissed. "Really?"

Despite my private thoughts, Brandon was shocked by my willingness to have sex. A stranger, someone he hadn't kissed, was asking him for a condom. What sort of girl is this? And when we lay down in bed, I was relieved I wouldn't have to explain. I'd refuse to see him again.

Brandon was doing me a favor. He was a bite of buttered bread in my starving belly. He was a one-off sexual partner in a sea of a future many. Once my "virginity was gone," I could date. I'd have flings, I'd explore desire. I'd be free. Well, free from everything but guilt. I expected the guilt to persist forever.

We kissed once or twice, but my focus was on the act. I distracted myself by staring at the bedroom door, counting slashes in the wood. (There were eight.) I knew the condom was unrolling over him, and I didn't dare look. I opened my legs and stared up at the ceiling.

I felt almost something but mostly nothing. Not to imply he was small but to say I wasn't present. I was thinking of how I'd tell Georgie and what David would say. I wondered if Jess and Michelle would notice a change in me. But when I got home, *The Real Housewives* blaring, Michelle shooed me away. "It's the season premiere." I floated to my room, noticing the sensation of wall-to-wall carpet beneath my feet.

Staying in the present was a welcome distraction. I couldn't bear the weight of my "sin." It was easier to focus on the sound of the shower and the heat of the water. I pretended God couldn't hear while I checked in with my body. Do I feel safe? Yes. Do I feel happy? Neutral. Am I hell-bound? No? I was surprised by the lack of guilt, the lack of shame. I'd made a choice that led to a moment and I was back home. Nothing had changed. Or, maybe, everything had.

ACT
2

6

IDOL

The evangelical church made an idol of sexual purity. Pastors and preachers built her an altar, brick by brick, and demanded we worship at Purity's feet. Teenagers paid penance for blow jobs and hand jobs and emotional affairs against their "future spouse." If you saw an eleven-year-old weeping in youth group, it's likely they'd touched themselves or kissed a girl. You know, those terrible acts of teen affection that will ruin the whole of society if not swiftly condemned by Purity.

Purity god is a pretentious do-gooder, veiled like Mother Mary but cruel like the devil, poising herself as the gatekeeper to God. "Oh, you gave to the needy? You read books to your grandma at the nursing home?" Purity doesn't give a shit. If you so much as thought about sex, she'd block your path to God. "He's super mad at you," she'd say. Then you'd get stuck apologizing to Purity, believing that the Father wanted nothing to do with you until you paid an exorbitant penance to her.

But back then, when I "lost my virginity," I believed in Purity god, idolized like a Roman deity (like Nike or Sol Invictus).

And actually: screw this. Let's call Purity a "he." Patriarchy begot purity culture, and evangelicals too often attribute evil to "she." Take Jezebel and Eve versus Kings David and Solomon. The former are evil; the latter are flawed. So guess what? The rest of this book is going to refer to this evil thing as a "he," just to switch it up.

When I would pray, I'd lean into my bed, on my knees, and beg for God's ear. I imagined acceptance of my request if I promised, "I'll stop having sex." Except that not having sex once you've had sex is almost as difficult as never having had sex at all.

I was supposed to regret losing my virginity, but regret was impossible. I was relieved by the freedom, by the hours of brainpower that would no longer be consumed by sex, sex, sex, sex, sex, sex, sex, sex, sex, sex, sex, sex, sex, sex, sex, sex, se—you get it. Now I could think of my friendships, my career, how I wanted to dress, and who I wanted to become.

The problem was, because Purity is an idol (a validated and worshiped idol), I didn't know who or what I'd be without my totem. My Christianity depended on Purity.

Single Christians are virgins. Virgins are Christians. But nonvirgins? Revelation 3:16: "Because thou art lukewarm, and neither cold nor hot, I will spew thee out of my mouth." Christians call each other "lukewarm" as an insult. If you questioned the authority of the church, of evangelical interpretation, you were "lukewarm." If you professed Jesus on Sunday but had sex Saturday afternoon, you were "lukewarm." And what happens to the lukewarm? Our all-loving Creator spits us from his mouth in disgust.

I was in hell. I was having sex on a semi-regular basis. I was no longer a Christian. Or, I mean, isn't that what an unmarried Christian is? A virgin? That's what Purity god had preached. But aren't Christians people who love and follow Jesus? I bit my thumbnail again. I guessed I'd forgotten the "follow" part. Because Jesus was a virgin. Right? Jesus's sexuality isn't discussed in the Bible, but we've all heard he was a virgin, like his momma. I threw a bathing suit in my over-sized purse and announced I'd be back in a couple hours. Jess waved from her computer, "Bye, babe!"

I flung my stick-shift Civic into fifth and cruised down the 101 freeway. I listened to worship music. "Our God is an awesome God, he reigns from heaven above with wisdom, power, love, our God is an awesome God!" I couldn't wait to drown these salty tears in the sting of chlorine.

When I talked to Georgie, my concerns didn't compute. "So, you believe me and David are going to hell for having sex?"

"No! Of course not."

"But you are?"

"Yes?" We stared at each other before I yelled, "Go!" Georgie and I liked doing laps at the Echo Park rec center. Her bathing cap had bright yellow latex flowers all over. I watched the blossoms disappear into the pool before I kicked off myself.

On the opposite end, Georgie asked me again, "So according to your religion, you're going to hell now? Because you had sex."

"Yeah, I guess."

"Well, your God sounds evil. Like, fucking evil. Don't you think?"

"No, he's not. I mean—"

"You're supposed to go swimming in a lake of fire because you have a crush on a guy? I mean, really?"

"Well, it's not the crush part."

Georgie rolled her eyes. "Go!"

Another lap, the other end of the pool. I said, "You're right. It all sounds weird."

"Yeah. It does. This is precisely why I don't care about religion." Georgie fancied herself spiritual but not religious. I envied the intuitive way she moved through the world. And I couldn't deny that I didn't believe God would send her and David to hell. So why would he send me? Because I loved him more?

I could defend God but not Purity. Purity god preached eternal damnation, but being sent to hell for consensual sex didn't resonate. At least, the literal place with horns and pitchforks didn't resonate. I was about to learn that hell is a place on earth. The tormenting fire is a state of mind.

✦◦✦

A year and some change had passed. I was a twenty-three-year-old unmarried woman in a sexual relationship.

Was I attending church? Yep. As far as Flowing Waters, Michelle, and Jess knew, I was a sexually pure lamb, white as snow. I'd sink in my seat when Jess called me a virgin. "Can you believe it?" she'd said to her best friend Kate. Kate was a pretty Aussie pursuing acting like most of us.

"Good on you," she said while Jess twirled Kate's hair around her finger. It didn't occur to me Jess was keeping a secret of her own. The duo were mighty affectionate, but so were a lot of girls. I'd have called Jess and Kate "touchy feely," but full-blown lesbians? No way. I was too self-absorbed to consider others' sins, anyway.

While Jess suffered the unique torment of being an "abomination," Michelle was pining for The One. We both believed that we might've ruined everything. Giving our bodies over to anybody but The One could jeopardize our destinies. I could get back on track with God as soon as I stopped having sex.

I read the Bible; I prayed. I avoided talking to God about sex. If I kept that subject off the table I could bypass the idolatrous god of Purity and make my way to the Father. "Please don't be mad at me," I'd beg before talking like He might still love me.

Meanwhile, my relationship with Flowing Waters was breaking apart. I attended Sundays but made an excuse to step down from the choir. If I were sinning, the least I could do was uphold the church's morality contract. Still, I'd ultimately end my relationship with the church once the pastor announced he was in favor of Prop 8, a statewide proposition eliminating the right of same-sex couples to marry in California. This anti-LGBT stance was no surprise. What was more disconcerting was to learn that the pastor opposed the presidency of Barack Obama because he feared the church would lose its tax-exempt status. In short, I felt he was opposing religious freedom and harming the LGBTQ community in favor of money. For this and other reasons I stopped attending Flowing Waters.

"Where were you?" Jess asked. I made excuse after excuse,

every Sunday. I was here, there, everywhere but church. Michelle said I was backsliding, and I knew she was right. It was bad enough I didn't devote myself to the weekly gatherings. Lord knows I was having sex and drinking too. Backsliding indeed.

People can have self-hating sex. Whether they're losing their religion or feeling unworthy of their partner, sex can lead to tears. After having sex with Brandon, I'd sit on the toilet, trying not to cry. I wasn't building this relationship on a foundation of self-love, respect, and mutual growth. I was trying to figure out who I was and what the hell I was doing. I regret to say, our relationship wasn't about him; it was about me. I was in my first sexual relationship and I devoted it to my pursuit of folly. I was shut off from my intuition and my Creator, running off the fumes of teenage hormones, ignited by the sparks of shame.

I never meant to get in a relationship with Brandon, but he'd pursued me, hard.

Brandon was on the road often and called me constantly. My cell would ring and ring. On the other end Brandon would demand my whereabouts. If I was out, he needed to know: "Who's there?"

"Me, Georgie, Sienna, and David," I said on one occasion.

"Who's David?" he snapped.

"Dear God." Sienna gasped once I'd hung up the phone. "He's being a psychopath."

I angrily superglued another ribbon to the top of a blouse. I was exhausted by Brandon's distrust. It was absurd for him to question my loyalty.

Sienna yanked the blouse away. We were prepping for a Pretty Pony shoot and she didn't want me to mess it up. "It's David, for Christ's sake." Sienna continued to prod. "Brandon knows who David is, right?"

Georgie beheld me with suspicion. I'd noticed a change in her demeanor since I'd begun having sex. She was comfortable with her *Clueless* Tai, a friend with no style and zero sense of the world. But I was coming into my own—like when Tai gets held at gunpoint in the mall and everyone wants to hear her stories instead of Cher's. Was Georgie growing uncomfortable with my newfound sexuality? Maybe I was a contender, someone who'd seduce her lover while pretending to be naive. But, God, that wasn't it at all! My best friends' boyfriends were like Ken dolls with hard, plastic lumps for penises. In other words, sexless. I'd never betray her or Brandon that way. And yet there I was, being accused by both.

I looked at Georgie, pissed off. "Of course, Brandon knows David. He just freaks out if he hears a man talking. A coffee barista in the background of a call—he goes off. I'm exhausted."

"I think he's cheating." Georgie said this so easily. Then she popped up, with no eye contact, and tended to the whistle of her boiling kettle.

"What?" Sienna plopped onto the chair beside mine. "Is this true?"

I was stunned and offended. What the hell? "Georgie?"

Georgie returned with a tray, a delicate tea set balancing on top, steam billowing from the pot. "Oh, don't look so serious." She could be cruel when drunk. I suspected she'd spiked her last two glasses with gin.

"Well, care to explain, G?" I loved that Sienna wouldn't cower for Georgie. She was no Barbie plaything; they were equals. They both had money, lovers, and careers. Sienna had nothing to lose, whereas my whole world would crumble without Georgie's affection.

Georgie doled out teacups and offered, "Sugar or honey?"

"I'm good." I was pretending to be unafraid like Sienna. "You think Brandon's cheating?"

"Bren, don't make me say this."

Sienna, David, and I leaned forward in our chairs.

"Brenda. You saw naked pictures on his computer. Of other women."

"I never liked him," David said. His defense of me angered Georgie further.

"Wait, wait. Hold the phone. Why am I just now hearing about this?" Sienna asked.

"Because it's nobody's business," I said. I stumbled around the table, gathering my purse and keys. "Have a fun shoot." And then, backing down, scared to lose Georgie over one fight, I added, "I'm not mad. I just wanna be alone." After I slammed the front door and walked down the driveway. Tears welled in my eyes while I considered my myriad of failures.

God, I was pathetic, having no style of my own. I lied when I was afraid. I gossiped when jealous. I asked too much and gave too little. I showed up empty-handed at dinner parties. I wanted to be an actress, but I scoured the city for agents and they said no, no, no. I was talentless, gutless, selfish, and had no clue what I was doing. It all made me cry.

Plus, Georgie was right. I found lingerie photos of some girl on Brandon's computer. He claimed Ivan—the band's lead singer—had hooked up with her. "Evelyn or something? Eve?" Ivan sent the pictures as a brag.

But this upset me more. "Why is he bragging about this bitch?"

"Whoa, settle down, Bren." It was the first time Brandon heard me cuss.

I glared at the girl, sprawled across her bed, in a bathroom mirror, in her car, selfies of this Eve being sexual and slutty. She wasn't afraid of hell, not that I could tell. I hated her. "Well, who the fuck is she?" I'd asked, using another rare bit of profanity. Brandon insisted he'd never met her, but I caught a weird smile. He looked pleased by the conversation. He liked seeing me jealous, I guessed.

Later, I blamed the fight on my NuvaRing. In a terrible bout of shame I'd ducked into a Planned Parenthood, hoodie up, and acquired free birth control. I was happy to have protection, but those hormones drove me crazy, once making me cry that a girl's hair was shinier than mine.

But we're off track! Lovers, listen! Georgie failed to mention the very reason I trusted Brandon, the moment he proved he was a faithful boyfriend.

Ivan and the band grew in popularity, with three hit songs on the radio and a feature article in Rolling Stone. Ivan was loyal to friends, hiring Brandon for each leg of the tour, across America and all over Europe. Southeast Asia was next on the horizon.

I was happy in Brandon's absence. With thousands of miles between us, I was rendered abstinent. In this chastity, the Purity god wasn't breathing down my neck and calling me garbage.

I didn't pray about sex, of course. If the Divine had a problem with my relationship and He told me directly, I'd have to stop having sex. I wasn't ready to make that promise (again). Instead I was blissed out, feeling like a real Christian. If Jess called me a virgin, it was easier to grin and bear it.

One night though, somewhere between Kansas and Ohio, Brandon called me, shaken up. "What's wrong?" I'd asked.

He explained that one night he jumped off stage, grabbed a beer from the greenroom and headed to the tour bus for sleep. Things were normal, he hadn't met anyone new, but he pulled the curtain across his bunk and found a naked girl lying there, smiling at him. "Nothing happened," he said.

I froze in fear, like a deer staring down the barrel of a shotgun. I knew I'd be blown away, but I couldn't move. "Nothing happened?"

"I promise." Brandon sniffled. "Nothing."

I asked why he'd bother to tell me then. I said I'd rather not know.

But he explained, "I want to be so transparent with you. I wanna be best friends and lovers, you know? I want to tell each other everything."

Georgie resented Brandon's confession, accusing him of trying to bleed intel from me. But I argued that I had nothing to hide. "And therein lies the problem," she'd said. "You have nothing to hide." She didn't believe a man on tour was capable of monogamy. "There's too much pussy. Anonymous, never-see-it-again, no-strings-attached, young, tight, easy pussy."

Sienna cupped her hands over my ears. "Don't listen to her. She's jealous we've got lovers on a world tour. And she's stuck at home with hers." You might have guessed—and it's true—that Sienna added Ivan to her list of lovers. Another famous man groveling at her feet. Ivan promised he'd be faithful, and Sienna laughed. "Don't be ridiculous. Live it up."

After Georgie's accusation, Sienna called Ivan and demanded answers. When I saw her next, she said, "Georgie's losing it. I told you. Brandon's been a good boy, cross Ivan's heart."

That settled it. Georgie was wrong.

Brandon was honest. Why else would he admit a girl came on to him? Why offer that information when he knew how furious I'd get?

From that moment on, I believed him. And though I appreciated my abstinence, feeling loved again by God, Brandon asked me to meet him in New York City. "It's fashion week, babe. Book a job."

"Okay," I said. Like booking fashion week were that easy.

Fashion weeks occur at least twice a year in various cities. And despite Brandon's faith in me, shows were not easy to book. New York, Paris, London, and Milan were showcases, not only for the clothes, but for the crème de la crème of supermodels. Fashion week is what you imagine: the celebrities, the fanfare, the nonsensical collections on Kaia Gerber and Gigi Hadid that make you scream. But what you may not know of is the existence of market week.

Market week, my loves, is the week after, when the fanfare dies down. This is when designers hire reps to peddle their clothes to actual stores to make actual money. After the boys with slanted backs walk for Gucci on the runway, a different crop of boys will parade a "ready to wear" version of those same looks for Nordstrom, Bloomingdale's, and others. Some styles live, others die. It all depends on which looks translate from runway model to Fifth Avenue housewife.

I'm in that second tier of models, never working the runway but always peddling the goods. And though market week is less prestigious, it pays a hell of a lot better. A girl could make $150 opening a show while I'd collect twice as much in half an hour. Runway models are expected to accept peanuts for exposure. And with no model union to protect the young and vulnerable, the majority get taken for granted, namely by our agencies.

Anyway, Next Models pushed, and I booked market week. And I wasn't an underpaid model. I had a booking and a free flight to see Brandon. I stuffed my suitcase with faux leather pants and sparkly jackets. I had enough boots for a family of four.

After landing at JFK, I headed for my friend's apartment. Tanya had once lived in LA, gallivanting around with me and Georgie. I missed her dearly. Last she knew, I hadn't had my sexual debut. Now she'd be meeting my bona fide boyfriend. When Tanya and I arrived at the Bowery Ballroom, the boys from the band, which we'll call "The Daring," were piling onto the tour bus. They'd finished sound check and would imbibe whiskey for a couple hours. I could see from a distance that Ivan was flying high, bags beneath his eyes after months of partying. Their tour manager, Phil, was present, exhausted and not excited to see me.

"Hi, Phil!"

He grunted.

"Are they on the bus?"

He looked dumbfounded, as if to say, "Are you blind?"

"Yeah, I see them. I'll hop on."

Tour buses gave me the same feeling as recording studios and Chanel runways. I didn't feel worthy of them. Which is absurd because, at the end of the day, we're talking about an oversized camper with dusty Venetian blinds. I planted my hand on the dining table and got my fingers covered in goop.

"What is this?"

Brandon appeared from the back of the bus, grabbed my palm, and licked it. "Cherry Coke."

I reeled. "Disgusting." But then we kissed. My body electrified. One month was like a million years, and I couldn't wait to sin again.

Tanya stood back, amused, watching the boys fumble through the tour bus like ants in an ant farm. They were toasted on alcohol and buzzed with excitement.

"The Bowery," Ivan said. "Can you believe it?" To Tanya: "I'm such an asshole, I'm sorry." He threw out a hand. "Ivan. Can I get you beauties a drink?"

"Absolutely," Tanya said.

Ivan wrangled shot glasses from the cabinet and crashed them onto the table. Jeffery—the drummer—caught one before it hit the ground. "Hey, Brenda." Our former "virgin" friend was going bananas on the road. According to Brandon, Ivan had to buy him condoms so he'd stop having unprotected sex. Jeffrey's guilt was palpable—and frankly dangerous—convincing him that to buy condoms would be to "pre-meditate sin." I'd heard that before, that Christians get STDs and suffer higher rates of pregnancy and abortion due to our masquerades of innocence.

I sat beside Brandon, sipping a drink, thinking, Holy hell, Ivan's a sex bomb. A true Casanova, he'd clock a person's desire and play into their attraction to him. He was like a bird in the wild, with tufts of vibrant plumage dancing and drawing in another lover. Once, he gently tucked hair behind my ear to whisper, "I can imagine," when I mentioned the difficulty of having saved myself for marriage. My instinct was to turn and kiss him, and even that resistance to my desire made me pulse. You know that feeling? The energy of you and another being, longing to meld into each other's bodies, that sparkly tingle that ignites into a flame the moment you kiss?

My crush on Ivan was major, but somewhat of a cliché. Everyone wanted him. That's why he was a star.

Meanwhile, Tanya waved her arms to let me know she was drowning. She was trapped in conversation with their bassist, Elroy. El talked endlessly about "gear." As soon as Tanya said she was a photographer, she got stuck listening to what sounded like the inventory list at B&H. "Help," she mouthed.

"Hi, Elroy," I said. "I missed you." I meant it. He was the kindest guy in the pack, albeit awkward.

The Daring members were single, aside from Brandon. I knew Sienna was still making Ivan cry, but his reaction wouldn't be a default to monogamy. He'd retaliate with promiscuity. I saw a Costco-sized tub of condoms on the bus. "At least you're being safe," Sienna would say, leading Ivan to fall between another pair of legs.

The Daring's greenroom was like any other. A foldout table was stacked with their rider: twelve Cherry Cokes, five bottles of Patron, two Tennessee whiskeys, Starbursts, Sour Patch Kids, three cheese pizzas, and a Caesar salad.

Tanya and I helped ourselves to tequilas with ice, because Ivan didn't get mixers. I scanned the table, and there was nothing healthy to eat. Tanya popped a Starburst and offered me one. Remembering the reason I was here—market week—I shook my head in mock devastation. "Oh, God, you're not going to gain five pounds in a day."

"I'm starving, but I can't." My anorexic days were over, but modeling required that I maintain an exact weight. A week prior, I was two inches too large to please this New York client.

I was a moderate drinker, but I was stumbling drunk in one hour. I hadn't realized how much less alcohol my body could handle without sustenance. Through the haze of tequila, I watched a "real model" plop onto Brandon's lap. They were both overtaken by laughter—and I could have murdered everyone in the room. I stomped over to my boyfriend and put my hands on my hips. "Brandon?" I glared at the girl, and she giggled.

"Yes?" she said. Her hair was teased to high heaven, her makeup done by a professional. She must've been a pro, booking fashion week, in lieu of its dingy cousin market week.

I shrank in shame. "Hey, I'm Brenda," and I met Brandon's eyes. His popped open, like he'd realized having a girl on his lap would get him into trouble. I caught Tanya squinting with suspicion.

"Oh, this is Evelyn."

Ivan's Evelyn? The naked computer girl?

"Eve actually."

My stomach sank. I was afraid I'd throw up. To see someone you love wrapped in another's embrace! Your blood temperature rises by a hundred degrees, and your knees buckle.

If you have the misfortune of seeing something like that in person, you're forced to play it off. You're not fumbling; you're dancing! You're not crying; it's raining!

God, it's awful.

I moved from one foot to the other, repressing fury. By now Brandon had stood up and kissed my face. "It's time," he said. The boys headed for the stage.

Tanya introduced herself to Eve, keeping our enemy closer. Eve gave her a dead fish for a handshake and skipped past, tiny gold shorts crawling between her cheeks. "Enjoy the show, ladies."

"I hate her," I said.

Tanya glared at the door. "I hate him."

⚭

After the show, we wound up at the Beatrice Inn. This bar in the West Village was elite, located in a basement beneath the street.

I couldn't deny the rush it gave me, to skip the line and strut in with Ivan. Back then, the paparazzi were becoming invasive, creating a feverish intensity between movie stars and their fans. *Star Magazine* convinced us to care about socialites, fashionistas, and London royals. We were "us," and stars were "them." Being close to successful people made me feel successful by proxy, while doing nothing at all. I could live off the fumes of that feeling for weeks.

Drunkenness helped me forget, and Tanya and I danced until Beatrice flung on their lights. On the street, the sun peeking up from the horizon, Tanya said she'd see me later. "Nice meeting you, Brandon." I watched her walk away, embarrassed she'd seen my emotions raw.

I blamed my lack of confidence for doubting Brandon. He called Eve a "supermodel," and I said she was hardly super. "She's not Jessica Stam." But he'd smiled and reminded me I'm a model too. I was obsessed with being pretty, like being the prettiest girl in the room would save me from infidelity. But Georgie once posted a meme that read, "No matter how hot the girl, someone's tired of fucking her." That freaked me out. More than this, as I fell deeper into a sexual relationship with Brandon, I'd convinced myself he was The One. I'd prayed for God to redeem my sexual sin and to clarify the truth: I was desperate to have sex, so Jesus had sent my husband sooner. Sure, I jumped the gun on the sex part. But if I married Brandon, I'd have slept with one person. I'd be a good girl again. I wouldn't be a lukewarm ho; I'd be a girl who slept with The One, a little too soon.

I could laugh about it later, like all the pastors did about their former indiscretions. "I was partying, you guys," says every tattooed evangelical pastor on earth, "but then, I gave my life to Jesus and he sent my wife, [Lori, Jen, Michelle]."

They'd continue, "She was sexually pure, and I'm so grateful for that. [Tanya, Kelly, Desiree] forgave me for my past and taught me how to be a better man." I'd look to said wife, searching her face for resentment, but it wasn't any use. All pastors' wives perfect the church smile.

Brandon guided me onto the bus, past the tub of condoms, which glared at me like a threat. Phil reminded us they'd be leaving in an hour. "Unless you'd like to wind up in Boston," he said, "I suggest you leave in thirty."

Brandon cowered, not sharing the clout of The Daring. "I'm a camera guy," he said to me. "I've got to respect Phil or he'll kill me."

I looked at Brandon's top bunk and heard Elroy snoring beneath. "Can we really have sex without waking him up?" Ivan was in the backroom, out of earshot. The situation was less sexy than I'd imagined. "I can't believe someone was waiting in here for you," I said, clocking his reaction, judging the mysterious "tour bus slut."

"I know, right?"

We managed to have sex but—imagine making love in a coffin or in a child-sized bed. It's not easy. But I needed to know that Brandon desired me. I needed to erase the sight of Eve on his lap. We fell asleep for a moment afterward, but woke to the engine roaring. "It's time," Brandon said, holding me closer.

My insecurity mounted as the bus pulled away. I was jealous of Ivan, that he was on an adventure and living like a king. I wished I'd been born a wild boy, like him. Hours crawled by at the fluorescent-lit showroom that day. I paraded outfit after outfit, distracted by a broken heart. I wasn't on The Daring's tour, and I couldn't be the prettiest girl in the room. "God, please protect this relationship," I prayed. "I know you hate me, but I want to do the right thing. I'll get married, just say the word." As if God had a vote in the matter.

In the following months, I spun out with this obsession—to wed and make things right. I continued to shake and cry after sex, in the privacy of the bathroom. Brandon knew I was a mess, and he did profess to love me. Once, while we made love on his bedroom floor, he said, "I love you. Oh my God, I love you." I wasn't certain I shared the feeling, but I knew our love could grow. It didn't matter that I was bored out of my skull when he dragged me fishing or to the garage to stare at his drift car. It didn't matter that when I drove to his home in Temecula my skin crawled, like I was headed in the wrong direction. It didn't matter that when we fought he couldn't see my perspective. All that mattered was getting right with God. I missed the love of my life.

7

ATONEMENT

Brandon asked me to marry him . . . on the rooftop of the Grove, an open-air shopping center. There's a slow-moving trolley and a fountain where tourists take photos flashing peace signs.

We'd been in an argument in the car, Brandon not understanding my pain. He listened to my frustration; he heard my torment around sex. Then he asked what marriage would mean. "Let's go back outside," he said.

Protective of his car, he'd parked on the roof. The setting wasn't ultraromantic but there was a view of the city. Los Angeles is hilly. From a height like that you can see lights twinkling throughout the mountains in several directions. It's strangely silent at that elevation.

Brandon and I walked to the edge.

I looked out, remembering the year I'd had. I was hiding from my family and friends, pretending to be the good girl I could no longer profess to be. I couldn't mask the truth any longer.

A few days before, I'd received a call from a hidden number. Private calls are either great news—like an invitation to an exclusive dinner—or a regrettable waste of time. I took the fifty-fifty chance, and it freaked me out: sex noises played on the other end. My heart sank to my stomach.

I'd been watching TV with Michelle, so I held the phone to my side and stumbled out of the apartment. On the other side of the door, I hugged the wall, my face flushed with fear. I listened again:

more sex noises. I started to cry, "Who is this?" Someone recorded me having sex with Brandon! How could I lie about my virginity now? "Who are you?" I demanded through sobs. Maybe it's the devil himself. (That was an actual thought.) "Who! Are! You!"

I look back now and laugh, imagining the person on the other end attempting a harmless joke. Probably someone I knew! And instead of giggling, I went running through the halls à la Drew Barrymore in *Scream*, gripping a carving knife like, "He's big and he plays football and he'll kick the shit out you!" It wasn't until I read Linda Kay Klein's *Pure* that I realized this type of irrationality occurs in purity culture survivors. This reaction, feeling as if my whole life would collapse because of having sex, is a part of religious trauma.

Brandon was being exposed to the cracks in my mental health, wrapped in the justification of "pleasing God." He was a secularist and not spiritual at the time. That was another reason we weren't aligned, but also he couldn't relate. When I relayed the prank call, Brandon was dumbfounded. "Who would film us, Bren? No one would. I promise." This misunderstanding began our fight in the car.

Now we were looking out at the city, wishing I were "normal."

He turned to me and wrapped his hands around mine. "What does marriage mean to you?"

Today the answer would be different—more expansive and not with the promise of "forever." But at the time I said, "It means two people supporting each other. Like, you and I both have big dreams. You want to make movies; I want to be in them. Getting married means that you're promising to do those things together. For the long haul."

"I want to support you like that."

Brandon was a kind, earnest momma's boy who'd survived a tumultuous upbringing. He had told me there was violence and infidelity in his parents' marriage. Some nights he and his mom would make a bed in the back of her station wagon. Being outside in the elements, mother and son, was safer than being inside the home with her husband. I don't remember when his parents parted ways, but I know that Brandon was the reason the violence stopped. What a heavy weight for the shoulders of a preteen.

That brave kid grew up into a good man. Brandon treated me with respect, he worked hard, and he always called me back. What more could a twenty-three-year-old want in a romantic fling?

"Will you marry me?" Brandon knocked me from my thoughts.

"What?" I scanned his hand for a ring. There was none.

Reading my mind, he said, "I don't have a ring or anything. I just realized: We should get married. You want to?"

I smiled, in awe.

"I will get a ring. I will."

I accepted. Brandon's offer was less of a wedding proposal and more of an out. It gave me the same sense of relief as hearing the math final got cancelled or waking up from a murderous dream knowing I wouldn't be doing prison time. I was burning in hell, and Brandon's marriage proposal was my ticket out. Which is why I speak kindly of my ex. He hurt me in the end, but he was trying his best. Brandon didn't want to be wed, but he'd sacrifice the freedom of his twenties to emancipate me.

Even if we didn't share a sophisticated love, his agreeing to marry me was a loving gesture indeed.

Within two months, Brandon found an engagement ring. He made decent money with The Daring and bought me something quick. A beautiful, platinum band from the 1920s.

A part of me thought, "I'm a gold girl. I hate diamonds. He doesn't know me." But these were presumptions I'd made about myself. Sure, I had preferences, but I was young. If you didn't count my mission trip to Ecuador, I'd only been to Florida, LA, and

Pennsylvania. I didn't know anything; that much I knew. I held up my left hand and let the diamonds catch the light. The rocks were placed in the shape of a daisy on both sides, the design asymmetrical, as if the flowers grew wild. It turned out, Brandon knew what I'd like before I did. I thought, "This is what marriage will be like: expansive." And it was—but not how I imagined.

But let's not get ahead of ourselves. Before a divorce, there is a wedding, and I certainly had mine.

When I was a girl, I didn't dream of weddings. I wasn't motivated by a distant day or the color white. I played with Barbies, but their story lines were intense, involving high-powered executive jobs and sordid affairs. My best friend Tara's mom recorded us playing in her room. Ken had cheated, but Barbie was too resilient to care. She wore neon business suits with strong shoulder pads. She had a pink convertible with cherries hanging from the dash. Her body was perfect, but—despite having it all—her divorce was inevitable. "Sorry," my Barbie voice said to Ken, "I just don't love you anymore." I suspected that relationships were more complicated than happily-ever-afters. By the time George from across the street cheated on Rose and left her (in a shiny red sports car), it felt par for the course. I'd heard all about men and their mid-life crises from Queen Oprah.

I'm perplexed now, knowing how cynical I was about wedded bliss. I mean, the cynicism itself doesn't perplex me. My doubting romance was inevitable. Every adult I knew was a divorcee. My parents were together, but on their second marriages. What perplexes me is how I was manipulated into revolving my entire teenage life around the pursuit of something I never wanted: marriage.

I try not to think about it often—the what ifs—but what if I'd never stepped foot into that evangelical church? What if Pastor Scott never told me that sexual girls must get married lest God spit us from his mouth?

When I was young I prayed every night, knocking my little knees onto the floor, begging for world peace. I had an intimate, intuitive relationship with my Creator. If I'd continued to trust myself, to trust that one-on-one relationship, would God have told me to get married?

I know—for a fact—that if I'd never gone to that church and if I'd slept with someone in the backseat of his car, I would have floated to the ceiling and gushed with God about it. "It hurt," I'd say. Or, "That didn't hurt at all!" Whatever the case may be. Even if the boy broke my heart I'd go to God, without shame. "I'm devastated, Father," I'd pray, crying into my pillow.

I would have talked to God about sex, but I don't know that my life would've been better for it without the presence of adults willing to educate and guide me. Growing up in a sex-silent household meant we had no rules around intercourse. There were no conversations about self-worth within intimacy. There's a chance I'd have found my self-esteem in people's beds. Even worse, my high school held off sex ed until senior year, and it was far from comprehensive. I could've gotten pregnant at sixteen.

Coulda been pregnant, woulda been happier, shoulda never met Pastor Scott—whatever—who knows? All's well that ends well, as they say, and a divorce is a happy ending if the marriage isn't right.

But—again!—we're getting ahead of ourselves. Before a divorce must come a wedding.

With the question popped, it was time to tell friends the news. Beforehand, however, I wanted Brandon to ask Dad for my hand. Dad is old-school, and I hated to imagine telling him myself, like he had no choice in the matter.

I wanted Brandon to ask my dad and, ever the planner, I fancied the timing perfect. My big sister Dawny was getting married (for a second time), and she was doing so in Las Vegas. The immediate family would be there, including me, Brandon, and Dad. I suggested my fiancé ask then, having no regard for the stolen thunder Dawny's virginal sister would suck from her big day. (Whatever! I'm twenty-three. Life is about me, me, me!)

The ceremony was sweet, with an Elvis impersonator presiding. Post vows, we stood outside as a family on the kitschy bridge of the kitschy wedding chapel. My thoughts shifted from Dawny to me, me, me. Brandon could ask my dad at any moment. When would he pop the big question?

I couldn't deny that none of this felt the way I'd dreamt it. I didn't dream about weddings, but I did fantasize romance. I thought my husband would be tall, dark, and handsome. That he was. But also he should be adventurous, spontaneous, and horny. Those were my top three desired traits. Brandon possessed none of them.

Intent—obsessed even—with atoning for my "sin" of sex, it never occurred to me Brandon wasn't "The One." Brandon had to be "The One" because I had sex with him. God knew I needed my husband, so he'd sent the guy. If there were growing pains in our relationship it was because Brandon was sent too soon. This disastrous union was my fault, every bit of it.

Back at the hotel, by the time Brandon leaned over Dad's bed and flashed him the ring, I was accustomed to disappointment. I got engaged on top of a parking lot, and now Brandon was asking for my hand in the laziest fashion. Hadn't Brandon seen a Disney cartoon or a Jennifer Aniston movie once, ever? He hadn't planned anything. I was devastated.

I swallowed a wad of spit—along with a myriad of emotions—and decided to be happy. "This is what you want, Brenda," I thought. I watched Dad's face light up. "Of course you can marry my daughter, Brandon." And as men do, Dad straightened up and walked to my fiancé for a handshake. "Good man," he said.

"Not really," I thought. But Dad was happy to see me happy. I was pretending well.

In old Vegas, we ate mashed potatoes and steak. Celebrating the newlyweds, Brandon and I played footsie under the table, copious amounts of wine having improved my mood. We were keeping our thunder-stealing secret on the hush.

Dad couldn't contain his excitement, however. He announced our engagement on a miles-long casino walk. "I hate this place," I'd whispered, watching the tacky carpet design repeat again and again, through a fake Italy, a fake Paris, a fake New York. "Oh look, the places I wish we were." I sighed, like a brat. I was lost in my thoughts until Dawny swung behind Brandon and me. She tugged on my left hand and glared at the ring.

"Is this for real?"

"Yes," Brandon said. I pursed my lips.

"When did this happen?"

"Well," I said, "here, but technically in LA."

She discarded my hand and took a sip of margarita from a teal plastic cowboy boot. "Come here." She yanked my arm and we sped up, leaving Brandon in our dust. "Where's the fire?"

"The fire?"

"I mean, what's the rush? You have your whole life ahead of you, Bren."

I was defensive but had no defense. What could I say? The God we both love will send me—but somehow not you—to hell if I don't get married ASAP?

Dawny looked at me, not wavering. "Where's the fire?"

"There's no fire." We were stopped now and the whole family stopped behind us. I pulled her closer, for privacy. "I just want to."

Incredulous, she threw a hand on her hip. "You want to marry this kid?" She had nothing against Brandon. Dawny demanded the truth. She knew that religion flung me into a world of guilt, and that Brandon was my first boyfriend. From her perspective, we must've been naive little kids, building a future as unreliable as a stack of Jenga blocks.

My stomach was in knots. "Yes, I want to marry him."

"Fine." She took a swig from her cowboy boot. "Brenda wants to marry him." To everyone in the casino: "She wants to marry him!" And we continued walking.

Dawny's reaction was bad, but my little brother's was worse.

"You're gonna marry him?" Kris's bottom lip quivered, and I could have died.

"Yeah?" I started crying. "Why are you crying?" We were two siblings on a bicoastal Skype call, blubbering like idiots.

"Because he's wrong for you, Bren. It's all wrong."

I wanted to freak out. Having suffered a year of inner turmoil, I couldn't now, at the bitter end, bear the truth: This marriage was wrong.

My body and my intellect were screaming, but I was taught to disembody. Spirit: divine; flesh: evil. Galatians 5:17: "For the flesh desires what is contrary to the Spirit, and the Spirit what is contrary to the flesh. They are in conflict with each other, so that you are not to do whatever you want." Therefore, my body had to be betraying me. She screamed "No!" but it must have been to sabotage God's will.

My heart screamed too, but I was taught to treat her with contempt. Jeremiah 17:9: "The heart is deceitful above all things."

Crying with Kris, I tried to build a case for Brandon. But Kris had nothing against my fiancé. Kris was motivated by love. He desired my happiness. He saw the pain in my future and cried ahead of time because there was no way to change my mind. He knew it.

Lucky for my stubborn behind, I was bankrolling the event. No one but me had a say. I decided to marry, and I was paying the price.

$\longleftrightarrow$

Moving in with my fiancé was romantic. We clinked wine glasses and looked out the large windows of our Sunset Boulevard apartment. Kids our age skipped through the street, hiding tequila bottles in oversized purses and making out. Without the impending doom of our nuptials, I might have enjoyed everything.

Tour was over and Brandon was home. We hung paintings

and set up a projector to play French new-wave movies against the wall. We had a one bedroom with a kitchen, living room, dining room, and an extra-long staircase. Our apartment was an upgrade from sharing a tiny room with Jess. When I moved out, she and Michelle hugged me tearfully. Michelle never asked, but still I clarified that I was a virgin. "It's gonna be hard to abstain, being in the same house, but I've waited this long, right?"

"Might as well," she smiled. "Making love will be worth the wait."

Meanwhile, life at home was excruciating. In another bout of paranoia, after we had sex on the living room couch, I worried we were visible from the street. I tried to remember which cars had passed by. Anyone I recognized? Would Ashley, Michelle, Holly, Phil, Harmony, Kenny, Bryan, Jamie, Lindsay, etc. etc. have seen us? It didn't matter that none of them had our address. I hid in the bathroom for a tearful shower. Shaky hands made it impossible to shave my prickly legs. I couldn't wait for the shame to be over. As soon as Brandon and I said, "I do," I could have sex in whatever window I wanted. Or could I?

Could we have sex in whatever window we wanted? That would be an immodest act. If a man saw us and jerked off, we'd have caused him to stumble (Romans 14:13). Instigating lust in anyone but Brandon would be a new sin (Matthew 5:27). I wanted to make sex tapes or have sex in the same room as a couple. I wanted to wear lingerie and dance through the house, having sex in every way imaginable. But I asked God, "Is that okay?" These were fleshly desires, not honoring to God. Pastor Everyguyever promised that sex within marriage would be a kaleidoscope of exploration. "God loves sex!" they said. Adding, with a forced laugh, "God made sex, guys. Hello! Me and my hot wife [Veronica, Aubry, Kimberly] have amazing sex!" But some people think missionary alone is acceptable. That stance is extreme, but those people do exist. You can catch them, five or so years into their "biblical marriage" in a sex dungeon, getting spanked and blown by a couple of doms. At least, that's a common enough outcome to have become a cliché.

In "biblical marriage" blow jobs are questionable—going down on your wife even more so. Female pleasure is a radical concept in both pornography and the church.

"God, are we allowed to do blow jobs?" My shower had taken a rough turn, from one point of shame to another.

Otherwise, I did enjoy sex a teensy bit more. At the new place, there was no accountability at the night's end. Michelle and Jess wouldn't be asking, "Where have you been?"

Brandon and I would have sex and spoon on the high thread count sheets. "I love you, Bren."

"Love you too."

◦─◦

Only a girl who never dreamt about weddings could survive my wedding.

Our wedding was a disaster.

First, venues were a challenge. I wanted a Diane-Keaton-shouting-off-the-veranda kind of vibe, but anyone in LA with a backyard large enough to accommodate a wedding is rich. I didn't know rich people, and if I had, I wouldn't expect they'd allow dozens of stilettos to trample their backyard to oblivion.

The garden party was a no.

You say, how about a museum or a gallery or a—"Sixty-eight thousand dollars? Ah, okay. That's a bit over my client's budget."

In LA, calling as a rep is better than calling as a nobody. (I've acquired night-of reservations at the Chateau Marmont with this tactic.) I was my own rep and learned that telling people you were having "a party" in lieu of a wedding cut the price tags in half. A wedding cake was $300. A "tiered cake" was $150. Chairs for "a party" included delivery whereas wedding chairs did not.

At last, brilliance hit. "It's a photo studio!" Brandon was amazed.

I found a guy who agreed to rent his photo loft for our wedding. The event began as "a party," but I gave in and admitted the truth. The guy, Zef, was going out on a limb. For $750 he'd allow us to marry on the roof and party in his loft. This was an incredible deal. Brandon and I toured the rooftop, walked to the edge, and reminisced about our engagement. "It'll be like the night I asked you," he said.

I pulled him closer and tugged his ear. "Perfect, right?" These were moments I thought we could pull off a happily ever something.

Brandon and I would be married on March 28, 2008. Tanya visited LA and photographed our invitation, which was in the style of Marie Antoinette. We rented king and queen costumes from a movie studio and teased my hair high enough for Sofia Coppola's approval. I borrowed Georgie's fluffy Pomeranian as a lap dog, fit for a queen. I bought an array of cheap cakes and plush fruit and spread them across the dining table. I got a turkey leg that Brandon could bite into. "Long Live the King & Queen!" the invitation read. People were so impressed; I'd find the postcard hanging on refrigerators years after our divorce.

My family flew in from Philadelphia, with Dawny and Joey notably absent. I wouldn't admit it then, but I had this flashing thought: "Why would they bother to come? They know I'll get divorced." I shook the truth from my head—with a literal shake—and kept moving. I had a wedding to plan!

I regret that I didn't check in with Brandon. Did he feel crazy too? Was he on my runaway train or tied to the tracks?

I expect that—if given the option—the average evangelical would say that marrying someone you don't love to have "sinless" sex is less offensive to God than having sex with your boyfriend. But let me tell you something. That's bullshit.

Pardon the French, but that measure of "sin" is complete and utter bullshit. Duping someone you don't love into marrying you—because you were indoctrinated into some deranged sexual ethic—is way worse than having sex with your boyfriend. Marrying someone you don't love is downright cruel. So I guess I was cruel.

The day of, Jess did my hair and makeup. We rented a room

at the Checkers Hotel, and my family and friends were scurrying around the suite, prettying up together. Georgie wore a tangerine dress with appliqué daisies around the collar. She snapped photos of me topless, in Spanx, on her huge Canon camera. "I can't wait to see The Dress," she said.

Sienna clapped her hands together. "Me neither."

Aunt Dori zipped the pretty Christian Lacroix I'd found at the Barney's warehouse sale, and the room filled with high-octave "Awwws." Mom pouted. "I can't believe my baby's getting married."

Georgie lifted the camera and snapped away. "Don't mind me," she said. Until then I hadn't wanted pictures. I couldn't relax. A pile of disasters had thus far haunted my wedding day.

First, the chair delivery guys refused the rooftop trek, citing legalities. Brandon had to take off his suit and haul chairs with Kris and The Daring.

Then there was the catering. I'd hired my wonderful friend Randy, a caterer I met on a shoot, who made the most decadent chocolate cake. I called him to relay the loft code and he said, "Oh, don't tell me now, darling! I'll forget by the wedding." He was supposed to arrive in two hours.

"So, you want the details, like, in an hour?"

His end went silent, and my heart stopped.

"You're, um, coming, right?"

"Brenda?"

"Yes?"

I heard Randy fumbling through his calendar. "Brenda."

"Randy."

Words need not be spoken. He'd written the wrong date. How much are 100 In-N-Out burgers, I wondered. Randy interrupted the thought. "I will be there in two hours."

"Are you sure?"

As though he'd been stabbed with adrenaline, he repeated, "I will be there in two hours."

We hung up.

As if things couldn't get any worse, there was a knock on the hotel door.

Knock, knock. Everybody froze.

"Who is it?"

Sienna turned the knob and found Brandon standing on the other side. I flew into the bathroom, avoiding the supposed bad luck of seeing a dress pre-ceremony. Jess and I holed up in there, and she brushed blush across my cheeks to kill time. "He looked worried," Jess whispered. He and I had gotten into a ravenous fight the night before. Brandon said things so unkind that I had my first panic attack.

I'd stopped by the Valley apartment to grab a few things I'd forgotten. I don't remember what the hell happened, but Brandon accused me of cheating and called me foul names. I thought, "I can't marry a person like this." But with my family in town, the loft decorated, the details in place, I couldn't imagine canceling the wedding. And for whichever of those reasons, I forgot how to inhale. Michelle held a brown paper bag to my lips. "Breathe, honey, breathe." When I drew enough air to speak, I explained that Brandon had accused me of cheating.

"Like, you're sleeping with somebody right now?" Jess said.

I nodded.

"That's insane."

Flash forward, back in the suite, Jess's wide eyes were looking at mine. Someone rapped on the bathroom door. "Yes?"

Sienna spoke. "Brenda, baby? Brandon needs a moment with you."

My heart stopped. By this point, Mom and her crew were headed to the venue. Going dark—as Depression-era poets do—I assumed they were dead. Or that at least one person was dead. I hope it's someone on his side of the family, I thought, pooh-poohing myself for being a bad person.

Finally I said, "Okay." I stripped off the dress and threw on the hotel's emblazoned robe. I opened the door and Jess scurried out. Once the door slammed, Brandon led me to the bed and motioned to sit down.

"Brenda?"

"Oh my God." I was terrified.

Brandon removed his hat, like when the police come to your door with the worst news ever.

"Oh my God, what?"

He pulled my hands into his. "Babe, I'm sorry to tell you this but—"

The expectation was unbearable. "What?"

"The rooftop. We can't get married there."

"What?"

"We can't get married on the rooftop. I'm so sorry."

"Who cares?"

"You do," Brandon said, but with a question mark at the end.

"No. I don't. I thought my mom was dead."

"What?" Brandon was alarmed, having a less morbid imagination than mine. "Everyone is alive. But we can't get married on the roof."

"That's fine." But, "Can we still get married?"

Long story short, the dude who rented us the loft didn't ask his landlord for permission. One hundred twenty people were meant to drink champagne on a rooftop, with no railings. The owner arrived angry. "There's no way this is happening."

"Are you serious?" Brandon was incredulous.

"A tenant jumped off a few months ago. This party is a wrongful death suit waiting to happen."

Ivan leaned in to butter him up. "Sir, it's a wedding."

The angry man glared. "Do I look like I give a shit about weddings?"

The boys hauled the chairs downstairs and into the alley, and my fiancé told them he needed a minute. Pacing back and forth, running hands through his hair, he prayed in earnest, for the first time in a long time.

Listening to this story, I smiled. I could tell there would be a happy ending.

Brandon said he paced though the alley, which was less of an alley and more of a court. St. Vincent Court, to be exact, in the jewelry district of downtown LA. Trucks backed into the stale street, which dead-ended quickly. On either side, there were shop facades that looked like a retro European movie set.

Brandon barreled past the facades, looked heavenward, and said, "Help."

"What's going on, man?" Brandon said that a homeless man, wearing white and named Saint Louis, tapped on his shoulder and had asked this question.

"He came out of nowhere?"

"Yes, Bren." Brandon told Saint Louis our predicament and—together—they schemed a plan. Saint Louis, Brandon, and the Daring boys replicated the roof layout but in the courtyard. They laid a knock-off Oriental rug on the cement where we'd say our vows. "Ashley's agreed to pull his trailer into the alley. So you can, like, hide in there until it's time to walk down the aisle." Ashley was our Burner friend with a 1970-something Winnebago. Ashley would drive the wedding party, pull the Winnie into the courtyard, and stay there for the ceremony. Dad and I would emerge from within. "Dum, dum, dum-dum!"

Optically, it sounded awful. "I'm gonna look like white trash." This was a common fear of mine, being from New Jersey.

Brandon grinned. "No, you're not. You'll look beautiful."

I gazed at him, softening. I'd dominated our wedding aesthetic, but Brandon had an impeccable eye. Also, what was the risk of surrender? My plan had proved a disaster. Maybe Brandon and Saint Louis were working with the aid of divine intervention.

"You promise I won't look trashy?"

"I swear."

And he was right. I see photos, and it's like we were wed on a movie set. The Winnebago looks strange enough to be bougie. Like I'm rich but I chose an alley location for the sake of being unique. When I emerged from Ashley's Winnie, Dad holding my arm, lights flashed like a sea of paparazzi. I saw Brandon's tall dad, but otherwise people were a blur. I was embarrassed to be the center of attention.

After the ceremony, at which Kris told jokes and my church friends Tony and Teresa (the cake maker) officiated, Earth Angel—a.k.a. Saint Louis—swept the court and ushered guests to the elevator. Saint Louis, Brandon, and I lumbered up the freight elevator, and Brandon pulled me close. "We're finally alone," he said, like he'd waited for intimacy. But I wanted my family. They lived three thousand miles away, and I missed them. Almost everyone I'd ever loved was in attendance, and I wanted to run to their arms, away from empty promises. I wanted to be an un-wed girl again, with no lies.

Lagging after taking photos, we got off at the eighth floor and the party was booming. Kris's friends manned the bar. Our projector played black-and-white films against the white brick wall. I dropped bright, red wine down the front of my dress after a clumsy hug. Onlookers gasped, but I didn't care. Looking back, I was on autopilot; I had checked out emotionally. To conduct the runaway train, with Brandon strapped to the caboose, I had to ignore reality. In reality, I was a newlywed, and this was my wedding. In anti-reality, I was getting unwarranted attention at an expensive party. It was too much.

Randy the caterer—God bless him—had improvised an exceptional meal. So I heard. The food was eaten—to the last half tapa—by the time I was through the receiving line. Missing the meal, apparently, happens to a lot of brides.

We danced, we drank, we held uproarious conversations, and I was the bride. My groom gazed from across the room, tipsy, with love in his eyes.

The crowd diminished two by two, then slew by slew until Mom, Brandon, and I were the last ones standing. The guy who rented the loft refunded all but $200, so we were $550 bucks richer. Saint Louis made a killing too, and we were glad that he did. People dug into their wallets and gave him $10, $20, and $100 bills. He was wearing white, from his painter's cap to his white canvas shoes. I half expected a pair of angel wings to rip through his Polo before he flew back to heaven.

I was exhausted, but on a budget the work doesn't end at the end. Brandon and I were obliged to leave the loft spotless. Past midnight, I swept the floor with a wide broom, in my Malbec-stained Christian LaCroix.

Brandon and I made our way back to the Checker Hotel. And, in the greatest irony one could imagine, we didn't have sex. "I'm so tired, babe," he said.

Brenda, the girl who "saved herself" for marriage—who wore the purity ring and gave a half-dozen avoidant HJs—didn't have sex on her wedding night.

The bed was soft and there were rose petals on the sheets. The double-headed shower would have to go to waste. I was disappointed, but I could admit I was tired too.

Plus, Brandon and I would make love for the rest of our lives. This one sexless night was not a bad omen. This was the beginning of our happily ever after.

8

MADONNA

Brandon bled from a father's wound that no woman could heal. I know it's a cliché, to blame dirty deeds on dirty dads, but clichés exist because they're often true.

If someone's a jerk, there's a root, a reason. But let's not confuse a cause with an excuse. We leave our mommas' wombs and crawl into this mess. The challenge of life is to navigate the violence—be it tangible or emotional—while maintaining kindness, lest we become the evil ones. Or, to put it more gently, the hurting people who hurt people.

Considering my husband's upbringing, Brandon's father was challenging to love. But Brandon's mom, Lil, I adored. She was my husband's cheerleader.

After her divorce, she kept a two-bedroom apartment off Camp Pendleton. Brandon's mom wasn't in the service, but she was military, working in administration at the base five days a week without complaint. She'd come home and stack fruit yogurts and baby carrot packets in a meticulous row. No matter how messy Brandon and I got, the house remained spotless. It was like Disney World, where maintenance workers track your every move so there's not a crumb on the pavement. Once, I made chocolate chip cookie dough from scratch, leaving an explosion of flour and a cracked egg on the floor. Dreading the cleanup, I broke for the bathroom, and when I returned it was like I'd never been in the kitchen, save the smell of baking cookies.

Lil depressed me because she kept her life small, on purpose. I hope she was happy, but I worried that Brandon's dad had turned her off to men forever. I'd beg her to sign up for Match.com or OK Cupid, citing my and Brandon's Myspace romance, but she refused. "I'm not going to spend my life cooking and cleaning for some man."

"You cook and clean all the time anyway," I said.

"Well, because I love you guys." She waved her hands as though shooing away suitors. "I don't need men." Brandon and I would visit and sleep over on occasion, and our presence lit her up.

My nagging doubts about us—Brandon and me—remained. No matter how sweet our time together, I had a sinking feeling I'd gotten it all wrong. Brandon should have been my first boyfriend. I couldn't believe he was "The One." And yet by my own blundered equation he had to be. Brandon was mine, forever.

Brandon was my only sexual partner, but he'd been encouraged to "bang" every woman he could before marriage. Women's bodies were used for pleasure, and their subsequent emotions were considered a joke.

I supposed it was better to break a slew of hearts on the way to the wedding chapel in lieu of cheating in the aftermath. But, lovers, using bodies is never the ideal, and that's not a strictly religious conviction. Even Drake croons, "Wish you would learn to love people and use things, and not the other way around."

When Brandon became sexually active at fifteen, he would be praised for "smashing" a girl—or two or eight. He could get a high five for a sexual conquest. The less emotionally invested he could be, the more "manly" he was considered.

Remembering these events, over a decade later, I have compassion. Men are often socialized to believe that promiscuity validates their masculinity. The more women "slain," the greater the man.

The tragedy—I felt—was that Brandon wanted to be faithful to a woman but that no one had taught him how.

While married, I preferred our cozy nights indoors. We'd run the projector and scour YouTube for psychedelic videos and Jodorowsky films. In the haze of sticky romance and red wine I could forget I'd taken a wrong turn. My gut clawed at me relentlessly, but after dark I forgot the day and enjoyed my husband. Wednesday nights were for sugary margaritas at Barragan's. Sometimes we'd walk over, but other nights we'd post up at our second-story fire escape, laughing at the drunk antics on Sunset Boulevard. Our neighborhood lit up nightly with energetic, horny babes and bike-riding boys wearing Chuck Taylors.

I loved to wake up at 3:00 or 4:00 a.m. for a pee. I'd tiptoe down the hall, reveling in our thrifted treasures and mementos from the wedding. I was proud to be an adult, chasing a dream in the heart of Echo Park.

Still, sex remained sinful, and I blamed the guilt-ridden sensation on my wretched self. I thought, "Sure, Brenda, you made amends. But now you're sinning by making the wrong decisions."

Ode to the evangelical torment: It wouldn't quit!

Once, our neighbors teased us for having sex in the shower, the sound of my moan traveling to their bathroom through the vent. We were meant to giggle for being caught, and Brandon did. I, however, was stoic and scared. Brandon's laughter sounded evil, like the devil waiting to drag me to hell. Purity culture has the power to convince us that even married sex is a sin if done the "wrong" way. My fears were irrational, but they felt valid to me.

Perhaps it was fortunate, then, that my husband and I rarely had sex. Month one, Brandon was consumed by a project, editing a video for TV On The Radio. His career blossomed through hard work, but mine seemed to stagnate. I wasn't lazy, but acting was difficult. The opportunities were few and far between. Flipping pancakes and gazing at the Hollywood sign from our kitchen window, my heart went out for myself. "Poor thing," I thought. "All this young, passionate babe wants is to have sex and to be an actress." But neither of those things were happening.

I was depressed and alone. So I killed time socializing. I befriended musicians, artists, and a few bona fide movie stars. I spent a weekend with a pair of famous starlets, eating their private chef's omelets and doing yoga with a personal coach. But this experience compounded my stress. I wanted to have a career myself. True gratitude was impossible in the midst of bright green envy and self-doubt.

What stirred my heart most was making art with Georgie. Georgie and Emily continued to shoot me for Pretty Pony, and I appreciated that the girls paid me fairly, like a real model. "Because you are one," Emily said, rolling her eyes. We'd go through stacks of soft shirts, pairing them with lace bellbottoms and gigantic hats. My makeup looked epic, but when I'd catch sight of myself I'd think, "I'm stuck with someone who won't make love to me." My beauty, I felt, was going to waste.

On a fall weeknight, Georgie was hosting one of her renowned sleepovers. Girlfriends gathered at her house and built forts out of floral sheets. We ate stemless cherries. We sprayed our hair with salt water so we'd look like land-bound mermaids. Georgie's soirees were pure magic. She was Francesca Lia Block's Weetzie Bat epitomized. She was playful and whimsical. Georgie was a whole skeleton made of creative bones. When I walked through the door of this sleepover, Sienna presented me with a tray of dirty martinis stacked with plump, green olives. I sat on the floor with our friends Mere, Chelsea, and Lisa, munching on an exquisite plate of crackers slathered in brie, honey, and sage. I nibbled cinnamon-roasted almonds while retelling the plight of my life. "He won't have sex with me."

Sienna danced to The Knife, which spun from a nearby record player. I was sex-starved and begging for the girls' advice. Sucking on an olive, Sienna said, "It can only be one thing."

Georgie sat down beside us. "You're Brandon's Madonna, not his whore." She drew a heart beneath my eye in liquid liner, without asking.

"Huh?"

"Exactly," Sienna said. She bit into a macaroon, gathering the energy to explain this trope. "Listen," she said. "You were once a whore."

My eyes widened.

"You're the opposite of a whore," Georgie explained, "but—"

"But!" Sienna pointed a manicured finger to the sky. "But! You were his whore."

"They call it the Madonna-whore complex," Georgie said. "Some men, they want the whore."

"You can spank, fuck, and lick a whore," Sienna said. "But a Madonna—"

Georgie interrupted, "Madonna is wifey. Madonna is the Virgin Mary. She's a woman so honorable, so pure that a guy goes soft thinking about her."

"Like she's his mother," Sienna said, biting into a chocolate-covered plum, twisting the figurative dagger in my heart.

Georgie collected glasses to freshen our martinis. "Either way, he's not fucking Madonna."

I frowned, my stomach in knots.

"Drink more," Sienna said.

But I was tired of drinking the anxiety away. "How do I become a whore?"

"Lingerie," Lisa suggested.

"It's worth a try," Sienna said. "I just hope he hasn't put you in the Madonna box. You're his wife, unfortunately."

"But what if I got filthy?" My sexual shame replaced itself with a competing evangelical ideal: the imperative to please your husband. "I'll do anything," I said.

Lisa poured a box of macaroons onto the carving board, and we nursed our martinis. I caught Chelsea's doe eyes, and they were wet with worry. She'd been at the wedding and had believed in our happily ever after. She dreamt of her happily ever after too, despite being single.

"Lingerie really is a great start," Sienna said. "What have you got?"

My panty drawer was admittedly pathetic, certain items being classifiably "granny." Maybe that was the problem. Not wanting to pre-meditate the sin of sex, I resisted buying the lacy, crotch-less, garter-buckled items of seduction. But that resistance was pre-wedding. I was four months a wife, and it was high time to seduce my man.

"Brandon has this Mad Men fantasy," I said.

The girls leaned closer.

"He said the secretaries, the 1960s thing, with the pencil skirts and sweaters, it turns him on."

"They all wanna be John Hamm," Sienna said, with a smirk. "So you'll be his secretary."

"Just not the one he marries," Georgie added. I took mental notes, hopeful that we'd devised a plan worthy of some good lovin'. While the party continued and my friends swung from room to room, scream-singing this or that Britney song, I spaced out. I imagined myself and Brandon having excellent sex, me bent over the kitchen counter with a pencil skirt around my ankles.

Come morning time, I sloshed peppermint mouthwash be-tween my cheeks and biked to the Sunset Goodwill. I found a fuzzy, mohair sweater and a plaid pencil skirt.

Ozzy Dots, the costume shop, was a block away. There, I bought garter belts and nude stockings with a pitch-black seam running up the middle. For $18.99, I was ready to buzz you into Brandon's office.

I smiled while I biked home, my excitement for seduction bub-bling over, like when you blow air through a swirly straw into a tall glass of Coca-Cola.

The following evening, I waited for Brandon to return home. At any moment, his cherry-red Vans would ascend the staircase, and I'd be waiting to pounce like a pretty kitten.

I wore the skirt and the yellow sweater, pinning a vintage brocade above my left breast. I lined my eyes with upturned wings, smearing the paint two or three times before perfecting the shape. I curled my golden hair and teased it to a beehive, best I could.

As I rolled the stockings over my legs, a jolt of electricity built between my thighs. "It's not a sin," I said. "Enjoy this." I took a rare hit of Brandon's weed to relax. I thought, "Baby, go easy. Look at your accomplishments. You're a traveling model, you're an aspiring actress. You live in LA, and your friends are total knockouts. Your crew is chock-full of creative genius!"

"And you're a wife, baby. You wanted this."

Looking in the tall bedroom mirror, black seams trailing up the curve of my legs, I thought, I'm beautiful. Fuckable, at the very least.

BAM!

At street level, our door flew open. Brandon slammed it shut. His huffs and puffs signified a long day. I knew he'd be exhausted. But I had good news: He'd be having sex!

We're socialized to believe that men won't deny sex. In the movies, a guy could return from his father's funeral, in shambles, but cup him between the thighs, and he's putty to play with. Men want sex, we're told. No matter what, no matter when, no matter who. With this belief, I strutted into the dining room and said, "Hey, mister."

Brandon had plopped his bag on the floor and was hunched over his computer, looking for a file. "Hey, babe," he said, without turning around.

"Mister," I repeated.

"What, babe?" He spun toward me in a frenzy, his hair messy like he'd been tugging at the ends. "I can't find this fucking edit."

Then, he noticed the Mad Men costume. "What's up?"

I shifted on my toes, feeling vulnerable and sexy.

Leading up to this moment, our sexless wedding night had proved less of a fluke and more of a preview. I came on to Brandon by kissing him, by lifting the covers to go down on him. But he'd pull me up and say, "Not tonight."

"Not tonight."

"Not tonight."

If you've been rejected, you know that the first few times confidence can remain. You buy the excuse that he's tired, he's full, he's drunk, and you try, try again. My pretty mouth will turn this whole ship around, you imagine!

But, by the seventh, tenth, and eleventh time, you may look in a mirror and blame yourself: I'm fat. I broke out. I'm a pest. I cried on the bedroom floor and he called me a drama queen.

"Why won't you have sex with me?" I said, "Am I doing something wrong?"

Brandon was callous and defensive, but that time he'd softened up. He met me on the floor and pulled my hand to his heart. "It's not you." This is what I told the girls at the sleepover. "I get turned off when you come onto me," Brandon said, "it's too much. Like, whoa."

"I'm too much for desiring you?"

"It's not your fault. It'll just work better if I come on to you." That was his guess.

I listened. I would stop seducing him.

Well, technically I'd stop.

I wouldn't make the physical moves, but I would light candles in the dark and sprawl out naked. When Brandon ignored me that time, I pretended to read a nearby book, to save the humiliation.

Tuesday, I bent over the oven, in an apron, with nada underneath.

"You're cute," he said, before slapping my derriere and returning to his computer.

This time, I thought, it will be different. He doesn't want his wife—the Madonna—so, I'd be the whore. I stood taller, gathering the guts. "Mister? I'm all done with my work." I was holding a manila folder with blank pages inside, going for the full effect. "Do you need anything before I clock out?"

Brandon grinned, to my delight. "You're done with your work?"

I could hardly contain my excitement. I was about to get laid! "My husband's waiting for me at home. But if you need me," I leaned over Brandon's desk, "I can do anything you like."

For a reason I couldn't comprehend, joy got sucked from the room, like when an impending storm is funneling energy into the air, readying for a clash of thunder. My back slouched in doubt. I snapped out of the fantasy. "What's the matter, babe?"

"What did you just say?"

I was silent. I had failed again and had no clue why.

"You said you want to cheat on your husband."

Dumbstruck, I dropped the manila folder. "What? How?" The folder floated away and scattered. I watched Brandon rush to the floor, crawling on his hands, gathering the blank pages.

"I don't need those," I said. My knees buckled and I met him on the hardwood. "I don't want to cheat on my husband. This was meant to be a fantasy."

Brandon grew indignant. "You fantasize about cheating on your husband?"

"I want to have sex with my husband, not cheat on him." Frustrated, I wiped a hand across my face, smearing the perfect cat eyes. "I mean, you! You are my husband, and I'm trying to have sex with you."

My husband stood over me, ominously, and handed back the manila folder. "That sucks," he said. "I'm taking a shower."

He walked away, and I waited—on my knees—for the bathroom door to close. It was like I'd been punched in the gut.

While saving sex for marriage, I fantasized about how glamorous my sex life would be. Ordinarily confined, abiding by the rules, these moments of ecstasy would release me. I just knew it. I pictured a pervy mate who would revel in my body over and over. But there I was instead, on my knees in a pencil skirt, humiliated.

The worst part would be removing dozens of bobby pins, one by one, from my beehive. I'd have to let Brandon come on to me from now on. I couldn't withstand another sucker punch to my self-esteem.

9

REVELATION

Drugs are a contentious issue on which I don't maintain neutrality. I have opinions. More than opinions, I have experiences— and profound experiences at that.

Growing up, my parents maintained a Don't ask, Don't tell policy on drugs. I preferred silence on the subject, but Dawny and Joey pushed the conversation. They blew weed into my crib to help me sleep as an infant. "No, you didn't," Dad said.

Dawny cackled. "Okay, Dad." Like, yes we did.

As for Kris, one afternoon he arrived home with a black eye. A classmate clocked Kris in the face for "no reason," he said, and I was furious. Later, my baby brother admitted he'd hustled a bag of not-so-magic mushrooms for $150. He caught a fist for it.

But I, Brenda, with the purity ring and extended list of Thou Shalt Nots, would never do drugs. Right? I was sober, and frankly I'd prefer to maintain that guise of innocence forever.

People knowing I do drugs embarrasses me more than people knowing I own a vibrator. Tightly wound inhibitions unravel with drugs, and therefore they'd render me vulnerable. The last thing I wanna do is roll my ass off and repeat one million "I love you's" to whoever used to change my diapers.

Besides the emotional exposure, drugs carry a stigma. No one wants the stigma. Which is wild because everyone does drugs. We simply judge people by their favorite drug's classification and whether or not they're taking something illegal.

Drugs are scheduled according to medical use and dependency potential. Heroin, methamphetamine, fentanyl, and oxycodone are wildly addictive and, dare I say, demonic, but two of the four are perfectly legal. I'm sure scheduling is a grueling, intensive process with a lot of good people behind it. But money is king. Drug manufacturers can afford to kill people and avoid prison time thanks to their pricey lawyers. When a person becomes sick with addiction, and the drug of choice (or rather, of necessity) shifts from legal to illegal, their family feels shame. Compassion extends until relatives lose hope and, with it, their loved one. Drugs can kill people.

Pop Adderall from your doctor or snort a line of cocaine. Either way, you're hopped up and vulnerable to addiction. Crush up said Adderall, snort it, and it hits harder. If it's a prescription, you've done nothing illegal. Having health insurance (and a shady enough doctor) means you've got access to legal drugs, even if they're killing you.

For Christians, our stance on the subject is presumed. By all appearances our answer would be: Just say no. But I imagine a number of parishioners at my church were hiding an addiction. If not an addiction, surely, the occasionally lit Saturday night. But while my pastors devoted sermon after to sermon to the supposed evils of premarital sex and rock and roll, I never heard about drugs from the pulpit.

Were we supposed to repent? And for what? Only powders and not pills? Or do we repent for pills but only the club kind?

I'm willing to bet a churchgoer's repentance was swift, but only if their drug use led to a true evil, like premarital sex or stealing. This is unfortunate because people ought to assess their drug intake to honor their mind and spirit. In lieu of vilifying our bodies to the point of disembodiment (believing the flesh to be evil and the heart deceitful), we ought to be checking in. Did you feel like garbage on Oxy, even with a prescription? Did MDMA inspire the most interconnected sex of your married life? Did you take acid and see "demons"?

In truth, substances can inspire or drag us to hell on earth. Some pills are addictive, and others can be a one-off. Some drugs encourage you to give them away, to share the joy with your friends. Other drugs coerce you into stealing from the ones you love.

Drugs are not bad across the board. They vacillate between good and evil, depending on the use. Drugs can facilitate healing or lead to destruction. Drugs reside in a grey area, but—as I've said—evangelicals tend to rely on a black-and-white binary. Like, legal is good, illegal is bad, case closed. But while we were married, Brandon challenged this assumption.

Brandon wasn't spiritual, let alone religious. His measure of good and evil was both nuanced and vague. While Brandon navigated the world with a haphazard and playful attitude, I behaved with militant restraint. I revel in the complication of grey now, believing grey areas to be the point at which we must press into God harder. But back then, dang, accepting the black-and-white answer to drugs was easy. Drugs were illegal and therefore bad.

Brandon himself smoked daily, saying he needed the calm of weed to edit. I respect that as his truth, but at the time I worried this was an excuse for copious drug use. He offered me his pipe and I declined, more than a dozen times.

Finally, I asked, "What does it feel like?"

Brandon smiled like the Cheshire Cat.

"Don't get too excited," I said, "I'm just curious."

"Well, weed is amazing." He spun his chair to where I was sitting, cross-legged on the shag carpet. "Weed's not addictive, but it helps me relax."

"Like?"

"Like, your body calms down. It feels like your blood goes slower."

"And in the morning?"

He widened his eyes, like a kid telling his favorite story. "It's literally impossible to get a weed hangover."

I reached out and he handed me the pipe. I didn't know how to work a lighter, so I bent down and he told me to, "Suck. . . . Now, hold it."

I froze.

"Exhale."

I did.

Sigh! That's the best way to describe cannabis, like a moment to breathe. My fear dissipated, as if the butterflies in my belly had fluttered away in a cloud of smoke.

Brandon was delighted. "So?"

I shrugged and handed back the pipe.

Brandon deflated and I headed to bed. "Goodnight."

I'd avoided telling him the truth, which was that I felt infinitely better. I worried incessantly about hellfire and work and money and relationships, but weed was a delightful little pause. The concern was that I'd seek this feeling forever. Mom said her stoner days made her complacent, but I remained motivated, wanting to work. I was myself, sans the anxiety and existential dread. When I tucked myself into bed, high as a kite, I forgot about fear and felt proud of my marriage. I was encouraged to be a good partner. I stirred from my attempted slumber and danced in the light of the projector, not worried about being spit from God's mouth. "Well, hello again," Brandon said. I smiled. I knew that God loved me— just because—like a good parent or a real friend.

"You were too high to feel his conviction," dissenters say. "And if you 'felt' good, beware. Those are your 'feelings,' Brenda. If you were led by the Word, in lieu of your emotions, you'd know that God hates weed."

I'd say, "I hear you, sister. I've heard it before." But you know that voice in your mind? The one that never shuts up? It's the voice that sounds like your own except that it's hell-bent on hating you? That's a voice I call The Antagonist.

"You look fat."

"God hates you."

"You're going to hell, bitch," The Antagonist says.

Cannabis didn't remove God's conviction. Cannabis muted The Antagonist. And in that precious silence, I heard God say He loved me and that He was proud.

Therefore, I got comfortable smoking weed on occasion. A researcher by nature, I googled "cannabis moral" for information. Turns out Christians were anti-weed, but I couldn't find a good reason. The argument was that we're to be slain in the Spirit and not messed up on drugs.

Fair, I thought, but being buzzed off a hit was hardly like being lost in addiction.

Respecting your temple was another point of contention for Christians. But I was intent on not creating a habit, which was very me. I drink, but I'm never hung over. I trusted myself to be exploratory but moderate.

Brandon and I would later try magic mushrooms, in Sienna's cozy and winding three-story house.

I was afraid to see demons, to be punished for being a bad girl who does drugs. But when the hallucinogen kicked in, Georgie and David looked like sticky kids, their lips stained in papaya juice. July had kissed freckles across Georgie's cheeks. David smiled pleasantly.

"What's so scary?" my spirit asked. "Why are you afraid?"

My fears bubbled to the surface as I presented them to God, one by one.

Afterward, I couldn't count mushrooms a sin either. I'd experienced an expansion and a release. I was spiritually healthier. I held closer to divinity thereafter.

⊰⊱

Now, don't get me wrong. Many times, once the high faded, my fear of hellfire tripled. In my black-and-white assessment I'd done something wrong. I had surrendered to smoking weed and to trying shrooms and, therefore, to the worry that I'd lost God's love.

Resisting The Antagonist, I wondered, if properly used drugs are not indeed bad—at least not across the board—had the church christened a mere cultural norm?

Nixon began the War on Drugs in 1971. Then in the 1980s Nancy Reagan popularized the slogan "Just Say No" to raise awareness of drug abuse. But our nation's anti-drug history is rife with racial inequality, the War on Drugs hitting minority communities the hardest.

As far back as the 1930s, billionaire William Randolph Hearst, infamous for his use of tabloid sensationalism, popularized the term "marijuana" to help Harry Anslinger—director of the Federal Bureau of Narcotics—vilify cannabis by associating the plant with Mexican immigrants. Anslinger testified before Congress, "Marijuana is the most violence-causing drug in the history of mankind. Most marijuana smokers are Negroes, Hispanics, Filipinos and entertainers. Their satanic music, jazz and swing, result from marijuana usage."

Nowadays our accused "satanic music" sounds more like Billie Eilish and Gucci Mane, but still: Are politicians and men motivated by the mighty dollar our best barometer for moral conviction?

We church folk say that, when sinning, you'll recognize your wrongdoing because the Holy Spirit will convict you. I worried this conviction would be harsh and cruel, but as I devoted myself to the pursuit of Jesus, I found conviction to be firm but gentle. A flaw of mine would pop into my mind, and I would face it, one dirty deed at a time.

I knew it was the Holy Spirit because God is love, and love was what I experienced, even when God called me out. For example, I once hated the apostle Paul. This is because Paul's scriptures have been misapplied to oppress and manipulate women and LGBTQ+ people. But when I said, "I hate Paul" aloud, I was struck in the gut by the loving hand of God. Conviction was nothing like The Antagonist. When God calls you out, you don't hate yourself. You course correct.

One of the problems in evangelicalism is that we've passed doctrine down, generation through generation, without much inspection. Our religious predecessors planted the seeds of an anti-gay, anti-women, pro-capitalistic church. From these seeds sprang evangelical doctrine. When you catch fire for Jesus and stumble into a dangerous church, you're handed the fruit of rotten doctrine and told it tastes delicious. Everyone around you throws their hands to the sky, thanking God for bruised bananas and moldy grapes, and you think, "Guess God isn't as loving as I thought." But you've caught the fire, so you comply with whichever biblical interpretation you've been given.

Interpretation, however, is an opinion, not a fact. We're meant to approach the Bible with humility in lieu of arrogance. When we deify the Bible, we risk growing numb to the soft ping of spiritual conviction.

Therefore, manipulation, unfortunately, can be exercised by good, God-fearing people. People who believe they're doing the right thing.

On the flip side, a person enticed by greed, sex, or power might use Jesus's name to justify their sins. Gluttonous people often read their Bibles upside down, convinced that a blessed life is marked by stock-market gains.

Faith curdles when the Bible becomes *The Wizard of Oz* and the church her Emerald City. When you peel back the curtain, you'll find televangelists who mirror Oz, the Great and Terrible, inflating their pockets, manipulating Christians through politics. The evangelical Oz pillages collection plates to buy a third and fourth house, to buy a second and third jet, while the poor go hungry.

That said, please don't grow offended, my conservative lovers. Right-wing evangelical leaders have used the Republican Party, but not because conservatives are evil. To the contrary, wolves in sheep's clothing sniff out our most earnest convictions and turn them against us. Wolves salivate, stalking places of power, opting for the ideology, religion, or political party that fattens them the best.

Therefore, we must ask ourselves, Why do I believe what I be-lieve? And, Have I been told the truth?

⚊⚬⚊

Brandon and I were together, as husband and wife, for two and a half years.

I hope I've painted my first boyfriend fairly—as a young, sweet, harsh, kind, complicated, resilient, confused, selfish, self-aware, hardworking gem of a person. By now, he was twenty-five and I twenty-seven. Little did we know, we were about to be single and set free.

My husband and I used to bike through our neighborhood. We each had a men's street bike with slim wheels and a bar across the middle. Mine was copper and maroon, and it glistened like those playtime motorcycles in a traveling fair.

One sunny afternoon we biked from God-knows-where, and Brandon, leading the way, pulled into a smoke shop. Brandon had a love affair with items, namely those with functionality. Weed pipes fell into this category—as did fishing rods, table saws, and literally anything at the Home Depot. Shopping with Brandon was my nightmare. I'd be bored out of my skull watching him pick up items, one by one, and draw them close to his face. "Does this come in red? Blue?" At Sport Chalet, he'd roll and unroll a sleeping bag ten times, with no intention of buying it.

Brandon was talking to the sales guy about the intricacies of blown glass and . . . I wanted to sink into the floor. "I'm gonna wait outside." I was hungry and thirsty and dying to go home.

Finally, he emerged from the shop, looking victorious. "Let's go," he said.

We hopped on our bikes.

Back at the house I cooked dinner. Mom raised a breakfast con-noisseur, but meals after 12:00 p.m. were cruel experiments. With fingers crossed I'd time the chicken, broccoli, and rice, but they'd finish in different intervals, burnt or undercooked. I was the queen of rice al dente and charred chicken. Often, I'd opt for a casserole or lasagna to thwart a timing disaster.

On this particular afternoon, while I agonized in the kitchen, Brandon was in the living room, relaxing on our yellow couch and packing a bowl. I brought out plates—pretty ones with painted birds—and placed them on the coffee table. I folded napkins and laid out the silverware, returning in a moment with dinner.

As I carried the steaming lasagna, I noted Brandon behaving strangely. He'd taken a hit and was leaning over his knees, silent.

"Brandon?"

His arms jutted forward, overturning the coffee table. Crash! Bang! Boom! Plates, candleholders, and silverware went flying through the air.

"Brandon?" I put the casserole dish on the floor and ran toward my husband. When I arrived at the couch, he was looking out the window, his eyes bulging, like they'd pop from their sockets.

I walked closer, wary. "Babe, you okay?"

Brandon stared ahead. His behavior was off-putting and scary. WTF was going on?

Then I remembered.

Off the cuff, when we left the smoke shop, Brandon mentioned he bought salvia. I had no clue what salvia was except that it was perfectly legal and available over the counter. (You may recall a Miley Cyrus video that surfaced around this era. She hit a pipe and was called out for smoking weed. Her defense was that the substance was not cannabis, which was illegal at the time, but salvia.) The researcher in me resented that I hadn't been warned or prepared. Brandon smoked a foreign thing and was staring into space, and I had no clue how to help. Would this high last twenty minutes? Four hours? My head was spinning, but at this point mere moments had passed, three seconds tops.

"Brandon?" I asked again, "Are you okay?" A bird dish crackled beneath my sneakers. "Ouch." Brandon looked up slowly, like a zombie. Then his eyes caught fire. That's what it looked like. His pupils were black and ravenous, alight with rage. I swallowed and stepped back. "Brandon?"

A sound left his throat, loud and definite. He said, "I don't know you," and took off, barreling down the hall. Unable to stand, he bounced off our furniture, reaching for anything to hold his body upright while he crashed through the dining room.

"Brandon!" I was yelling now, afraid for us both.

He paused and he calmed a bit, pressing his hand against a credenza for support. "You are not real," he said.

I felt foolish reasoning with him, but I tried, nonetheless. "Don't worry," I said. "I'm real. You're safe."

"No!" And he went running again, crashing into the walls. "You are not real," he said, pointing at me before falling to the floor. I knelt beside him, and he looked above my head, at someone I could not see. "I'm coming," he said.

"Oh my God. What?" I cried more. "What's happening?"

"You. Are. Not. Real." And again, to the unseeable thing, "I'm not taking her. I'm coming." He stood up and continued crashing against the walls, yelling, "She's not coming!"

I wasn't offended. I knew he was on a drug. But who was he talking to? Ghosts? Demons? "Tall, iridescent aliens," he said later. "They were blue." In Brandon's mind, once he'd taken a hit of salvia, our second-story apartment tumbled to the ground, like in an earthquake. It was the end of the world, and Echo Park was on fire. As he moved through the halls, his imperative was to leave the house. The blue aliens were walking in a single-file line, up to the distant but visible Hollywood sign. When he ran to our bedroom and ripped off the screen, he put one leg over the sill of the open window, ready to step out. "The house collapsed," he said, "so in my mind, the pavement was right there."

I wiped tears from my eyes. Brandon's trip had lasted eight minutes, and in that time he'd managed to tear through the house, destroying our things. I'd used the weight of my body to pull Brandon away from the bedroom window to save him from falling two stories.

There was a pounding at the back door. Our neighbors yelled through the wall, "We called the police! Brenda, are you okay?"

I looked at Brandon, mortified. "We're fine."

Later that night, we processed the event. I swept broken dishes off the floor. My favorite one, with a sweet canary, had shattered beyond repair. I stepped into that mess, but my foot was saved by a sneaker. "I'm glad you were wearing those," he said, pointing to my Adidas.

I emptied the dustpan into the trash, fuming. "You didn't tell me you were taking salvia."

"I'm sorry."

"I was scared." I hesitated, reaching for the courage to ask, "Why did you say you don't know me?"

"I don't know," Brandon said.

I was suspicious. He'd answered too quickly.

"You can tell me anything." I sat beside him on the couch. "You said I wasn't real."

He pulled my head close to his and sighed. "I don't know why I said that. I was high."

But a few nights later, he told me the truth.

<hr>

Ephesians 5:13 says, "But everything exposed by the light becomes visible—and everything that is illuminated becomes a light." Sitting atop a pile of shoes, pondering this verse, I wondered if the Bible was right. Could things be better in the light?

Surviving Brandon's Madonna-whore complex was a feat. My lover took my body for granted one hour into our marriage, and it hurt. That's why I set to cooking and cleaning and working out. I aimed to improve myself and become desirable again. After all, Pastor Everyman told us that men were insatiable for sex. Men cheated because wives weren't bringing their A game. Based on this intel, my marriage would thrive if I could just be better.

My friends complained about having too much sex, Sienna admonishing a woman for wanting it in the summertime. "She didn't even have a fan," she said scowling. I couldn't believe the heat was enough to put her off. I would satiate a man easily, I thought.

Ever since I can remember, I've been terrified of being cheated on. As a naive kid, it wasn't the physical act that worried me. I was more concerned about being played for a fool.

When Brandon admitted to cheating, the news coursed through my veins like ice water. Betrayal felt exactly as I'd imagined. I remembered my childhood neighbor Rose and how she'd cursed her ex, with his shiny, new lover and his cherry-red convertible. Rose's fury scared me, but I thought, That's appropriate, I'd be pissed too. And I was.

Once Brandon told me the truth, I began ripping off my clothes before locking myself in his closet. My reaction hearkened back to biblical mourning, when devastated men tore at their own beards or ripped their robes to shreds. I considered this while noticing the jab of dress shoes, Vans, and Doc Martins digging into my derriere. "Come out of there and talk to me. Please," Brandon said.

"No."

I'd been duped. I was a fool. That story from The Daring's tour bus, the one where the girl presented herself naked in Brandon's bunk, had ended differently. In its original version, my fiancé was disgusted that a girl had come on to him. "I told her to get out," he'd said.

I pictured the girl scurrying from the bus, humiliated, and I giggled at her plight. "Good," I'd said. "She deserved it."

In reality, however, she'd received what I'd been begging for. I found it strange that Brandon had gone out of his way to fabricate a happy ending.

Brandon pressed his face to the closet door. "Listen." He explained that when the salvia-induced, iridescent aliens entered our home—and his psyche—they'd told him I wasn't real. "You, of course, are real," he said. "But our relationship is bullshit. I based this whole marriage on a lie."

I hated to know the details but demanded them anyway. "Was it that fucking slut, Eve?" She deserved my rare cussing.

"Evelyn."

I peeked from the closet. "Oh, fuck off."

Brandon clamped a hand over his mouth. "Shit, I'm sorry."

Brandon and I spent weeks rehashing his infidelities. I asked for clarification over and over, demanding answers to irrelevant questions like, "She was fully naked?" I wanted to know, "Could Ivan hear everything? Elroy?" We'd hung out with the band days before. We drank and laughed together, and I couldn't believe they harbored a secret from me.

"Ivan tried to talk me out of it. He loves you."

Brandon said he'd slept with two-and-a-half women. "What's the half?" I said.

"Well, the last time, I did ask the girl to leave. We didn't have sex." I guessed this meant he'd performed sex acts that didn't involve penetration, as if this were a consolation.

Drugs, despite their legality, are not black and white, even when their nature is extreme. Drugs bring agony and ecstasy. Drugs often reveal hidden truths, and the truth is powerful, however you get to it. I'm not saying drugs are biblical, but again, Ephesians 5:13: Darkness is illuminated by light. Within that illumination, within that revelation of truth, we can make informed choices.

Drugs—vicariously—had changed my life.

10

LIBERTINE

I wanted to be a forgiving wife, but Brandon's affairs were heavy. It was as if he'd been carrying a backpack full of bricks and said, "Here, you carry this."

That's how it went. Post-salvia, Brandon was up in a frenzy at 3:00 a.m. He shook me awake and said we needed to talk. On tour, he hadn't been in his right mind, he said. Brandon had made poor decisions. He had cheated, he said. "I'm so sorry, Bren."

This is when I went running to that closet, ripping off clothes like I was going someplace I wouldn't need them. I can't say I've sat in a closet before, but it felt like the only escape. The sexy pictures on his computer flashed through my mind. Evelyn's boobs, Evelyn's butt, Evelyn's lingerie.

Brandon's sneakers beneath me were like a pinch. The shoes said, "You're awake. You're not dreaming."

After he passed this pain to me, Brandon got a pep in his step, like his agony had lifted. We'd walk to the Chinese market for mangos, we'd order deep dish at Masa, and he'd be smiling, happy that our love was now "real." "Because I told you the truth," he'd say.

"I've been telling you the truth the whole time." Did he want a consolation prize for becoming honest, four years into our relationship?

"I'll never lie again," he'd say.

I'd squint and try to believe him.

They say once a cheater, always a cheater, but Brandon was in agony, gripping my waist and begging for forgiveness. It was hard to imagine he'd choose to revel in this pain again.

On the other hand, why had he told me? Georgie believed he was unkind for coming clean. His objective was selfish, she said, to alleviate his guilt. "If he really loved you, he'd keep his mouth shut. He'd suffer in silence." But I disagreed. Deceitful secrets rot and curdle in the dark. Only truth can diminish the power of a lie.

Still, The Antagonist tormented me, playing elaborate, erotic films in my mind. I saw Evelyn expertly bouncing on Brandon. The Antagonist convinced me that the band counted me a fool.

The Antagonist reminded me that if I got a divorce I'd have wasted everyone's time. My parents flew from Philadelphia, my dad walked me down the aisle, and for what? The Antagonist wet his lips and whispered, "You dragged them three thousand miles for nothing. They'll hate you."

The Antagonist was lying, of course, lying being his expertise. In truth, our friends and family were happy to celebrate our union, even if it wouldn't last. Also, Ivan told Brandon that he was the dumbass, not me. "She's a catch," he'd said, "like a mermaid. Don't throw her back to sea." Ivan found me a rarity, having been with only one man. People were often stunned by my "purity." Even Phil had warned Brandon to be wary of my religious lean. "You're the first dude she's been with, man. She's gonna want more experience." When he saw Brandon's lip quiver, he added, "Or not."

The idea that I'd desire someone else scared Brandon shitless.

But he was right to be afraid now. After he admitted his indiscretions, someone else was precisely what I wanted.

———◆———

You might say my sex life was ironic.

I saved myself for "The One," but "lost it" with a stranger.

I lived for the promise of wedded bliss but didn't have sex on my wedding night, or much thereafter.

In honor of the irony that marked my sex life thus far, I planned to fix our marriage by breaking it further. To be a great wife, I'd need to have sex with someone else.

Brandon buried his head in his hands. "What the fuck, Brenda?"

I shrugged.

He paced the room furiously, yanking on his hair. "What. The. Fuck. Is my life?"

I didn't care how he felt about this proposition—or rather, this demand. He searched my face for compassion, but I had none, not for him.

The night prior, Ivan had come over and we projected *Das Boot* onto the wall. I remember nothing of that movie, except for a beautiful Charlotte Rampling . . . and the bunks. In a submarine, men piled into their sleeping quarters, and my heart stopped. I imagined Brandon and Evelyn in one of those bunks, sharing a million orgasms on the bus. I glanced at Ivan, and The Antagonist reminded me of his complicity. "Excuse me," I said, before darting down the hall with tears in my eyes.

In the back bedroom, I flung sheets over my head and hid, like a kid in a homemade fort. Brandon knocked on the door. "Come in."

He sat on the edge of the bed, wringing his hands. "What can I do? I don't know how to make this better."

"Then go away." That backpack of bricks, the one I was hauling, got heavier. Brandon's relief brought me pain and—worst of all—I was meant to forgive him.

Brandon was my first sexual experience, and I had vowed—before friends and family—that he'd be the last. "I do" meant I'd be with Brandon, sexually, for the rest of my dang life. But Brandon slept with girls prior to our relationship, then added to those numbers on tour. Those women before me I could handle, but more?

Sienna had a scary theory. "What if he told you to stop himself from doing it again?" I wondered if Tour Slut was calling or if he'd kept Evelyn's pictures. "Infidelity is erotic for some people," Sienna said. "Secrets can be sexy." When Sienna said so, I resented that I had no secrets of my own. I wanted a secret—or five.

Frustrated, I'd walk laps around Echo Park lake. Without the accountability of Jess and Michelle, I wore the teeniest shorts and slimmest tees, sans bra. This haphazard style—though alluring—was a sign of my naivete. I didn't intend to be seductive. And the summer was hot. While monogamous, I had blinders on. I didn't notice or care when men desired me.

With Brandon's admission, however, the scales fell from my eyes. My husband wouldn't make love to me, but here, at the lake, I saw men desiring me, licking their lips. I became like Eve in the garden, folding arms over my chest, noticing my nakedness. I saw my favorite thigh mole exposed.

It was after this stroll that I stomped up our stairs and demanded to have sex with somebody else. "ASAP." I bit my tongue in lieu of adding, "I saw twenty prospects in the park."

When Brandon emerged from the shower, his eyes were swollen and dark. I handed him a glass of water with Advil, like a 1950s housewife. He leaned on the counter and took a breath. "Look—"

I sucked my cheeks.

"We will figure this out. If this is what you need, we'll do it. Could . . . could you just tell me what you're talking about?"

"Absolutely." I had a plan. "You've had sex with a lot of people, Brandon."

"Sure."

"I'm worried that if I don't have sex with other people—even though you did, while we were together—"

"Okay—"

"—that a screw will come loose. I'll drown our kids in the tub, or run away to Paris to have sex with a trillion Frenchmen."

Brandon lifted his hand like: Enough.

"The point is, I need this, with or without you." And here, I offered three options. "One, we invite someone over, and you let him—"

Brandon turned green. "Got it."

"Two, I disappear for a few days, and you don't know where I am. Poof! Disappear. Then, I come home, and we never discuss it again."

"Or?"

"Or"—last option—"we get a divorce."

"Jesus."

I'd reached in the backpack and handed back two or three bricks.

"This is killing me."

"Yeah, it hurts." And I left for another walk, feeling lighter.

Brandon was in hell, but me? I gained my footing, for the first time in my adult life. His infidelities freed me to confess a long-hidden secret, so hidden that I hadn't even realized it myself.

In order to be with one person—and to go unquestioned by dissenting voices—I'd pretended that "saving myself" had been my desire. But in fact, I was merely responding to the guilt trip placed on me by pastor after pastor. The secret was, I desired sex with many people. I wanted to have sex with a hundred people, or a thousand. As a teen, before I met Purity god, I'd imagine kissing the beautiful actor Paul Walker and then the cute boy behind him, and the cute boy behind that one. Before Pastor Scott, no one had told me it was a sin to desire, nor to desire in excess.

Brandon's truth, that he'd cheated, made me determined to settle the score. That was a decision I made out of fury. But when I considered the exploration, the dance of seduction with other men, I swooned. His betrayal had somehow negated the potential to "sexually sin." Having sex with other men was a means to save my marriage. How could God fault me for that? It was like my militant abstinence had been at the top of a pendulum. Brandon's news broke the tie, and I went swinging to the other side, wanting sexual liberation.

Our first step toward "healing" was a night on the town. Believe it or not, we made a grand time of it . . . at first. Brandon and I chose our outfits together, switching one dress for another and these shoes for those. We made out and fooled around, turned on by the idea of prowling around, looking pretty.

We walked to the—dare I say—best venue in LA history: M Bar. Brandon and I took a seat and sipped our cocktails. He was a whiskey man, neat. "Should we order anything to eat?"

"Nah, I don't think so," I said. I was eyeing the long-haired boy across the bar. He had sullen eyes, wore black leather, and was oh-so-aloof. "He looks interesting."

"Him?" Brandon frowned. "Are you serious?" He pointed. "Him?" and I pulled his hand into mine.

"Chill." I smiled. "He'll catch us."

"Catch us doing what?" The mood was changing, and with it Brandon's mind.

"Babe." I smiled playfully, hoping to remind him we were having fun. But when I caught a whiff of his rage, I backed off. "Look, nothing needs to happen tonight. We're just teasing. No rush."

"But him?" Brandon sat back. "He's disgusting."

"Well, I didn't get to choose your exploits, did I?" Whenever Brandon got hurt, I'd remind him he deserved it. Like, hey, this is your fault. Remember?

"You're being cruel."

I looked at the boy, this time not masking my affection. The grimy babe smirked and sat an inch taller.

"I'm going to the bathroom." Brandon headed past the grand piano in a huff.

Aha, now the boy and I were alone. I puckered my lips and gave him the cold shoulder. Without the remotest concern for Brandon's well-being, I wondered how we might get him home. Would it scare him to be propositioned by a couple? Would he be turned on or repulsed?

I was inconsiderate and maybe, like Brandon said, cruel. I wasn't practicing mutuality, autonomy, or sexual integrity. For a nice Christian girl, I was sure sinning.

I define sin—quite accurately according to Jesus—as that which causes harm. We evangelicals made moral lists when it came to hand jobs and blow jobs, but we never ever talked about sexual integrity. It was all, "Say no, no, no ... wear a white dress, say yes!" Meanwhile, I don't believe "sinless sex"—a.k.a. sex that causes no harm—can be achieved without viewing sex through the loving lens of sexual integrity.

Sexual integrity is nuanced, complicated, and calls for intimate conversation. Purity god, however, slips beautifully into the binary, and Purity was all I knew.

Purity says that girls are either bad or good, pure or impure, based on our "virginity"—or lack thereof. Purity god blames "sin" for sexual incompatibility, and he doesn't bother to equip us for the horrors of life.

Since the #MeToo movement began, Purity's accommodation for the victims of sexual assault was to say, "Yes, the rape made you impure, but that's why Jesus died, to make you pure again." With that sort of rhetoric, Purity god proves himself a heartless little shit.

Purity god is so rotten that he's even convinced some God-fearing men that marriage is irrevocable consent. Can you believe it? Unless your wife's sick—and not that "headache" lie but truly sick—she can't turn down sex. Purity wags his finger and says, "Ephesians 5:24: Therefore as the church is subject unto Christ, so let the wives submit to their own husbands in everything." Controlling and insecure partners have this half-verse memorized, of course. And let's be clear. Using the Bible to force compliance would be the opposite of sexual integrity.

The second, less popular part of Ephesians 5:24 is this: "Husbands, love your wives, even as Christ also loved the church, and gave himself for it." Although this verse wasn't written in the context of sex, Ephesians 5 sermons taught women that our sexually charged, male counterparts would be insatiable. We'd spend our marriage meeting his needs. "Wives, submit."

Meanwhile, hello. Desire isn't gendered. Many women— believe it or not—want sex.

I've heard pastors—male and female—suggest that husbands do the feminine chores, like washing dishes or vacuuming the floor, to inspire sex from their wives. "*That* turns me on," says Pastor Everywoman. Which has since blown my mind because— though acts of service are a valid love language (one of five)—if the church promoted female pleasure, I believe it'd be a hell of a lot easier to get godly women into bed. Then sexual submission could be reserved for its only valid purpose: kink. Kink over coercion. Just sayin'.

Ironically, in purity culture, women aren't even taught that they deserve pleasure. Despite God creating the clitoris—which serves no other purpose except female pleasure—I've never heard a sermon about our sexual desire. Women are painted as hypersensitive beings, wanting sex only for its emotionally connective quality. Pleasure-seeking is reserved for the men, and for the Jezebels, like me!

The sad truth is, Purity god doesn't want pleasure. Purity is rotten to his core, his aim being to incite sexual violence, sadness, anxiety, and shame. Purity is not a man. He's an oppressive system, chock-full of people, good and bad.

As we wake up to Purity god's ill intent, we may scapegoat and blame him for our church's rape culture. But if you're the arm of an oppressive body—deeming preteens pure or impure—you're a part of purity culture, no matter how insignificant you perceive your role.

If you don't take issue with Purity, if you believe him to be fair and just, you're not looking hard enough. Purity god and Jesus are not one and the same. As a matter of fact, they're adversaries. Lovers, I beg you to pivot and see what God—the real one—has to say about your sexuality.

When Brandon returned from the bathroom, I was ready to seduce the grimy babe across the bar. It didn't occur to me that guilting my husband into my own revenge sex would be a violation of my husband's body and spirit. Being a student of purity culture—a broken-hearted one at that—I didn't possess a sexual ethic that honored God. Being taught nothing but "Say no, no, no . . . wear a white dress, say yes" left a gaping hole in my sexual understanding. "Consent," "mutuality," and "autonomy" weren't words I'd ever heard of, let alone understood.

That lack of sexual integrity, beautiful people, was my sin, not my sexual desire.

Brandon's eyes filled with tears, and my compassion kicked in. As selfish as I'd been, I didn't aim to hurt anybody.

"Let's go home," I said.

To this, Brandon agreed.

In a last-ditch effort to save what was broken, we attended a sex party.

When I tell people this story, they're shocked and amazed. I've shared the details with three or four friends—which for me is discreet—because attending a sex party was a leap. I'd jumped from sex with one man forever to an orgy attendee, overnight.

After our disastrous evening at M Bar, conversations between my husband and me evolved from vague to explicit. We realized that to forge ahead, without hurting one another, we'd have to get specific. We had no knowledge of "sex positivity" or "enthusiastic consent" as buzz phrases, so we went off instinct. That instinct told us to be clear and kind.

Over brunch at Millie's, we agreed that Brandon wouldn't enjoy a threesome. He said, "I'd rather you do that on your own. Maybe stay at Georgie's or something. Get it out of your system." From what I recall, the mimosas hit hard. He wasn't ordinarily this calm about the situation.

I appreciated that Brandon would explore with me, and I let him know it. "Of course, babe," he said. Then, sadly, "I love you." Opening up our relationship under duress was not an honest exploration. We were avoiding a breakup. We'd been married two years and, dang, even though I wanted to bail, we'd traveled fast and far on this runaway train. Why stop now?

As a rule, I try not to be careless with people. I'm careless with phone screens and wine glasses, which are perpetually broken, but I'm careful with hearts. If my words sting, I assess their meaning. I ask whether repentance is required or if it's the person's perceptions or Shame that's come knocking.

In this case, I dragged someone to the altar. Brandon gave me his life, till death. Biblically speaking, a divorce was reasonable (see Matthew 19:9). But I had spoken vows to God and taken them seriously. Our marriage deserved a shot.

I told my friends he'd made a mistake but was a better man for it. I guarded our marriage like a hound, promising people I was happy—not to be deceptive but so they wouldn't worry. Besides, I knew I'd survive. I maintained an undercurrent of fury just in case I needed the anger to propel our divorce.

When I suggested a sex party, Brandon chewed chilaquiles and needed a moment. I teased him. "Are you gonna choke?

"No." He took another swig of champagne. "I'm down."

"Are you serious?" I was over the moon.

Brandon was careful to downplay his intrigue. "Anything for you."

When we got home, I ran up the stairs and googled "sex party Los Angeles." Of course, an extravagant *Eyes Wide Shut* caliber party wouldn't be easily accessible. We wanted assurance that the attendees would be sexy and smart.

"Isn't there anything VIP? Can you ask Georgie?"

I reeled back, horrified. "This is our secret. We're not telling Georgie." I imagined word reaching my friends—people peripheral to this mess—who wouldn't understand the situation. I was behaving irrationally. The last thing I wanted was a voice of reason.

"Okay, well, how do we find a decent sex party?" Brandon was engaged, bringing chips and salsa from the kitchen and sliding into a chair. I'd found a site that looked promising. No blogs, no links. There was simply a keyhole on a pitch-black screen. Click the key and your messenger pops up.

Brandon and I stared at the screen. "Well," he said. "What do we write?"

I bit my cheek and typed. "We are discreet, respectful, and open-minded." That's good, right?" Then I attached a photo with our faces cropped out.

"Don't send that. They'll think we're hiding something"

"No, they won't." I hoped we could gain admission, from the neck down. I couldn't float a sexy pic on the internet. My religious trauma kicked in and I imagined Michelle flashing the invite-me-to-an-orgy pic on the screen at Sunday service. Michelle would have no way of knowing we were attending a sex party, nor would she shame me in real life. "But," The Antagonist said, "what if she knew you'd be looking for a sex party? What if she created this site as bait, to prove you're a bad person?"

Was this rational? Hell no. Did I proceed as if the Michelle conspiracy theory were true? Yes.

Neck-down picture it was. I pressed send and Brandon deflated. "They won't know if we're hot."

I leaned in to kiss his neck. "They'll know, baby. They'll know." Then, I took a steaming hot shower, feeling happy for the first time in a long time.

The day of the orgy, Brandon and I shot a music video. The shoot—as all shoots do—ran late. Around 7:00 p.m., I was wringing my hands, dying to race home and get ready. When we wrapped, Brandon flew down the 101 and got us back to our bedroom. We picked out my clothes together, settling on an ivory miniskirt, silk top, and—ironically again—my rose-colored wedding heels.

At a warehouse beside LAX, we watched the planes hang low and take off. After surrendering a $100 bill at the double doors, we were pointed down a long hallway. The bass of electronic music shook the walls. Brandon grabbed my hand and squeezed. "This is crazy," I said. We were giggly and nervous.

On either side of the hall were doors, and in each doorway a different scene. A subway station, a classroom, and a doctor's office—with the stirrups. Wow. Brandon loved the secretaries of Mad Men, but Roger Sterling was my fantasy—aggressive and bossy. I grew wide-eyed while perusing an unoccupied office, equipped with a desk and chair. "It's like playing make-believe!"

"Let's keep going," he said. Brandon slung an arm around my waist and led us deeper into adventure.

After seeing the empty playrooms, we found ourselves in a large room with a dance floor and a DJ. I couldn't believe it, but there was a buffet too—which I've since heard is a sex party standard. Shrimp, cheap sushi, and crab legs. "So much seafood."

Brandon bit into a chicken tender. "I know."

We were uncomfortably early. Guests hugged the walls, boozing up and making small talk. I was disappointed by the pot-bellied guys and by how many more men there were than women, but we soldiered on. Surely, the *Eyes Wide Shut* crowd would be fashionably late. Brandon grabbed a plate of chicken tenders and we went for a walk.

The venue was a sprawling warehouse. There were empty rooms with a round bed each, wrapped in rubber sheets. Whoever owned the venue had built walls for pseudo-privacy and peepholes for voyeurs. Upstairs, we discovered a cavernous space with black pleather on the ceiling, floor, and walls. Instruments of consensual torture stood proudly, taunting or seducing guests. There was a cross to which you could affix someone's arms and legs. There was an array of bondage pieces, painted black, looking stolen from a high school gym. "Is that a pommel horse?" A brave couple began their night, lightly electrocuting a woman in a latex cat suit. Brandon looked at me. We ran away wordlessly.

An hour and a half passed. People began having sex, but I found their lovemaking grotesque. The sounds of their bodies were awful to me. Slap! Slap! Slap! No one was moaning or screaming in ecstasy. Whether observing or being observed, the sex didn't appear to bring pleasure.

The bodies involved were imperfect, but that wasn't the issue. The crowd was alienating, and a few men leered, objectifying me. Maybe you're thinking, "Yeah, dumbass, it's a hedonistic, evil sex party." But wasn't there supposed to be a fairy orgy godmother somewhere? Someone to create healthy parameters and lead this orgy into consensual ecstasy? Men hovered over the buffet, and their girlfriends looked dissatisfied. I began to wonder who else might be there under duress or false pretense. Frankly, we didn't seem to be the only couple present hoping to fix our relationship.

Desperate for a break, we headed to the roof. The rooftop was arranged with clean leather couches and sleek firepits. I'd found a high-end party, but my desire was dry. "Should we leave?"

Brandon lit a cigarette. "Don't you want to have sex?" he said. "Maybe let people watch?"

I pretended to gag. "No."

Brandon sighed. "Let me finish this cigarette."

Then, like a pair of angels careening down from heaven—or ascending from hell, depending on your view of unwed sex—a couple approached us. Brandon fumbled with his lighter and the girl offered him a flame. "There you go," she said, looking down at us in her pretty lingerie.

My heart stopped.

"Mind if we sit?" The man beside her was tall and handsome. He wore a smart suit, and she, a lace bodysuit with garters.

Brandon moved over and offered his seat. The man settled in, crossed his legs, and took a peek at his watch. The girl presented her hand, like Brandon was meant to kiss it. He did. "I'm Stella."

"Aurora," I lied.

"Brandon," he said, blowing our cover.

"Are you having a nice time?" Stella twirled her blonde hair and leaned close to me. "This is my boyfriend, Ford."

He sat back and beheld me. "We're happy to meet you."

Stella was at ease, despite being younger than me. She popped her gum and put a hand on my knee. "Do you want to get out of here? We're leaving."

Ford added, "We don't want to go without you."

This proposition required no discussion. Brandon and I skipped down the stairs like deviant little kids. We were off to play make-believe with others!

Ford's place was a trek from the warehouse at LAX. Brandon drove his loud, yellow Beetle and we sat in silence, following Ford's pearl Lamborghini up, up, up, into the Hollywood Hills. After weaving for twenty minutes, crawling higher and higher into affluence, we pulled into a long driveway and my stomach flipped. We waited for the chrome gate to lift.

I stood and gazed at the house until Stella's boney fingers wove through mine. "This is Ford's baby. He built the place from scratch."

"Beautiful."

Ford led us in and tossed his keys by the door. "Don't brag, baby," he said.

"I won't brag, daddy," she teased, before clicking a button that slid the back wall of the house wide open. Stella winked, like, Amazing, huh? I nodded. Without the back wall, there was a clear shot of the entire city. An infinity pool kissed the edge of the mountain.

"Holy shit," Brandon whispered.

I shushed him while Stella walked over holding fluffy, white robes. "I don't imagine you brought bathing suits."

"We didn't," I said. "Thank you."

"Drinks?" Ford stood behind a chrome bar, stirring an old fashioned. He christened the rim with an orange slice and passed it to Stella.

"Sure," Brandon said. "Rum and Coke?"

"I'll have an old fashioned." Brandon looked at me like, Since when?, but Ford seemed pleased. I felt my face turn pink.

While Ford fixed our drinks, Stella disrobed on her way through the living room. Soft, dirty blonde hair met the arch of her back and I envied her for having no tattoos. Stella looked back at Brandon from the twinkling pool and we watched her figure disappear, limb by limb, into the water. "There you are." Ford gave us our drinks. "Let's go."

We wound up in the hot tub, the bubbles masking our nakedness. Stella popped out of the pool and leaned in to kiss me. Accustomed to kissing rugged men, I found her softness strange. Her tongue was plump, and she smelled like roses, or gardenias. I didn't like her touch or her pheromones.

"Would you like to kiss Ford?" she asked.

"No," I said, surprising myself. I looked at Brandon and the awkwardness set in. I felt bad that Stella turned me off and that I didn't want Ford touching me. I tiptoed through a minefield of emotions, realizing that Brandon and I couldn't swap lovers without blowing up our relationship.

Stella and Ford remained at ease, but they sensed something was amiss. These people were experts in seduction, from the mood lighting to the strong drinks. I felt we were duping them, present only to save our marriage. I felt guilty that they were forthcoming and we were full of it. With sexual integrity, Stella asked, "Is this okay?" before making any moves. "Can I touch you here? Can I kiss you there?" she asked.

Steam rose off the pool, but the weather was crisp. I shivered, upset.

"Let's go inside, shall we?" Ford suggested we warm up by the fireplace.

Sensing our trepidation, Stella suggested an activity. "Why don't you and Brandon have a bit of fun in front of us? We'd love to watch." So, my husband and I kissed. I breathed, relieved that Stella had removed herself from the picture. In the familiarity of my husband's touch, I was turned on at last. The breeze tickled my naked body. The fire warmed my skin.

Sensing a shift in my mood, Stella made a request on her boyfriend's behalf. "Aurora, would it be okay if Brandon touched me? Ford would love to see that." Stella was sweet and gentle, seemingly void of coercion and enjoying herself.

I caught her hopeful smile and said, "He can touch you." Brandon reached out his hand and began pleasuring her, but with that, energy sucked from the room like the devil had inhaled it himself.

I sat up. "We have to go."

Stella jumped. "I'm sorry!"

"You're wonderful," I said. "It's not your fault." And that was the first true thing I'd said all night.

My awareness had peaked the moment Brandon's fingers

touched Stella. I knew that I'd dragged Brandon into my own ploy for revenge. There, Brandon wasn't welcome to pleasure. The sex party, the other men, had all been my attempt to even the score.

As we drove down, down, down the hill, I knew. If Brandon and I stayed married, I wouldn't rest until I hurt him back.

ACT
3

11

SEVERANCE

This would be a great place to say I made the difficult but necessary decision to divorce. I ripped the Band-Aid off our bloody marriage. I left wounded and beaten, but dammit, I did the right thing.

This would be a great place to say that.

This, however, is a story about me. Sloppy, confused, twenty-seven-year-old me. I was prepared to buckle down and drag this unholy union on forever.

"Burritos or Thai?" Brandon called from the kitchen.

"Order whatever." I was watching myself on an audition tape. "I don't care." I glared at my shirt on the screen, imperfectly tucked. A stray wisp of hair was sticking straight up. "Oh no."

Brandon met me in the living room. "Thai in thirty. Plus mango sticky rice."

"Cool."

Brandon reached for the laptop, and I let him take it. "I'm pressing send, okay?"

I gritted my teeth playfully. "Yes."

"'For I know the plans I have for you,' says the Lord." I wanted to become an actress so badly, to have a positive impact on the world. I imagined myself on Conan, legs crossed on his couch, slapping a hand on my knee when he teased me for being a Christian. "Oh c'mon, Conan! I love Jesus and I'm not ashamed of that." I was going to make Christianity cool and accessible, breaking its ties to bigotry and hate. I wasn't sure yet if being gay was a sin (it's not), and I knew dang well that purity culture had screwed me over. But I'd practiced loving sinners, like the unwed Georgie and my bisexual best friend Sienna. Hell wasn't for them. If I won this movie role, I'd be one step closer to spreading the Good News among my peers, and on a global level.

"For I know the plans I have for you." Every time life seemed to move, or to mirror my fantasies, I assumed my God-given destiny was on its way.

When I wasn't modeling, I was taking jobs as a stylist's assistant. I'd climb the ladders of Universal Studio's costume house and scour for "football-loving father of two" or "wife with a naughty secret." Styling was fun because the job came with descriptors. My boss Ellie could say, "Bowie-esque alien" or "dad in a midlife crisis," and we'd find the clothes to suit that character. You may forget to appreciate attire while watching a movie, but clothes provide the subtext for a story or tell a story of their own. Styling requires skill and finesse.

The stylists I knew were these diminutive, overworked, impossibly chic girls who ran pounds and pounds of wardrobe. I watched Ellie swoop up a box that must've weighed the same as a twelve-year-old girl, her thigh-high Hermès boots clomping through Universal. While lugging this imaginary world she was creating, she mentioned her boyfriend's movie, which was in preproduction. "You know, Billy is casting *Adventures in the Sin Bin*," she said. "Are you still acting?"

I stopped in my tracks. I wanted to book a movie, desperately. I'd swapped agents twice that year and hadn't experienced an ounce of success. "Yeah, I'm still acting." God? Is this my destiny knocking?

Like it was nothing, Ellie flipped the monstrous box into her trunk and said, "You should audition." I wanted to scream, Yes! But this proposal would require some prayer.

As an evangelical, I had a myriad of fears about my body. I loved acting in school plays, but Pastor Scott would ask, "What's the line between what you do and what the character is doing?" Jim Caviezel—who played Jesus in *Passion of the Christ*—became a symbol of self-restraint, promising he wouldn't compromise and kiss anyone who wasn't his wife, even for a film. After hearing this, I pondered the line between art and real life. If my character were to sin sexually, would I too be sinning?

Brandon and I read the script that evening. The writing was witty and cute, a coming-of-age tale inspired by John Hughes. Billy wanted me to play That Whore Kim. She was a high school senior who had a reputation for being a "whore" but—plot twist—she was a virgin. After the last page, I turned to Brandon. "I love it."

"Well," he grinned, "you've got this. It's basically you."

That Whore Kim and I did have notable similarities. We were naive. We were hesitant to possess the sexual power we'd been given. We both quelled our sexual frustration by flirting and pre-tending to be someone we couldn't be. Kim pretended to be a whore and I pretended to be a happy wife.

Of course, I liked that she was a virgin. I fancied that plot twist as her moment of redemption. The role would require an oral sex simulation, but I imagined that Pastor Scott, Michelle, Jess, and Pastor Everyman would forgive my action, portraying a virgin giving head for the greater good of a story. The lesson would be: There's no shame in being a virgin! Amen.

It took a few months for Billy to call with the news. "The role is yours!" He and the writer, Chris, had me on speakerphone to enjoy my electric reaction, but I was too shocked to emote joy.

"OK," I said.

I could almost hear their excitement fizzle.

"Do you want the role?" Billy asked again.

Despite the lack of inflection, I was beside myself with joy. I forced a cheerleader's "Absolutely!" Booking *Sin Bin* was a dream come true. I'd not only booked a movie, but it would be on location, in Chicago. I'd be hired as a local and would shack up with Billy, Ellie, and our other costume designer—my friend—Marissa.

Before my flight, the beauty department consulted me on becoming That Whore Kim. In my mid-twenties, I'd have to somehow present like a teen. To do so, the hair team suggested bangs. When a cheap stylist in Silver Lake cut the fringe too thick, I was horrified. "I look like a nerd, Brandon." Eight years out of high school and I was still afraid to be uncool.

My husband kissed me on the lips. "You look perfect, Bren." And with that, Brandon drove me to LAX—joking about when we were last there, "Slap! Slap! Slap!"—before dumping me on the curb to catch my flight. This would be my Day One, and I'd be running to wardrobe as soon as I landed.

Friends called me "the queen of Pitchfork(.com)" because I co-starred in music videos galore. This, however, would be my first speaking role. "A-hem." I got on my own nerves, clearing my throat again and again and again on the plane.

When I landed in Chicago, I chugged a bottle of water and walked out of the corridor. Reminding myself to be confident, I whispered, "For I know the plans I have for you," before waving to my driver. Never before had a person been waiting for me at the airport, holding a sign.

"Brenda?"

"Yes!"

The driver was a young intern. He looked like a hopeful golden retriever, moving shaggy hair from his face before chucking my luggage into the trunk. "That's Steven," he said, motioning to the man sitting shotgun.

"Steven," I repeated. "I'm Brenda." And then he turned around.

I felt a ZAP! between the thighs. Our chemistry was palpable. I took a whiff of his scent: yum. His hair was slicked back, unmovable in the wind. "Right?" he said.

I came to. "What?"

"I'm just saying it's great to be in Chicago."

I rolled up my window. "I couldn't hear you."

He grinned. "Anyway—"

We three talked about the weather—literally—until we reached Steven's hotel. I watched him walk away, step by step, then the intern dropped me on set. While Marissa scurried us to wardrobe, I asked, "What's up with Steven?"

She playfully rolled her eyes. "Oh God, everyone's in love with him."

"He's hot."

"Yep." Our conversation was matter of fact; Marissa had been at my wedding and took my inquiry about another man with a grain of salt. After all, I didn't think about cheating. Steven was alluring. Whatever. "We all think he's hot."

Marissa led us into a high school classroom, and Ellie opened her arms for a hug. "It's That Whore Kim! I'm so excited." She out fitted me in tall, white knee socks and a schoolgirl uniform, with a push-up bra. She strung a gold cross around my neck. "Because all the religious girls are sluts."

I laughed. Ellie knew I was a supreme "good girl." She was teasing.

When the girls pushed me onto set, people clapped. "Oh my God," Billy said. "You're Kim."

I lifted my skirt and curtsied before hitting the electrical tape mark on the tile floor. In my first scene, I'd be trash talked by the lead actress, Emily Meade. I didn't know it then, but Emily would become one of my very best friends. She's gone on to break hearts in HBO's *The Leftovers* and *The Deuce*, but at the time she was "the girl who commits suicide in *Boardwalk Empire*." That's how I bragged on her when I booked the movie. With that as her descriptor, Sienna swooned. "I love that girl. Give her my number."

Emily's character was jealous of mine. I was the bombshell and she the manic pixie dream girl (as if that's so bad). She was meant to hate me in the script, but I noticed that her plump Joker lips would frown when I approached her on set. I asked Marissa if art imitates life. "Does Emily hate me?" In reality, she was concentrating on her work. The pout was nothing personal, but the less attention she paid me, the harder I tried to woo her.

As for art imitating life, I played Kim and she played me. She and I were intertwined. I watched the crew gawk at my push-up bra. I bent over to pull up my knee socks. I was a clichéd sexual fantasy—naughty schoolgirl—and was loving every minute, pretending not to be me. I began to lean into men's desire and flirt. Sure, I was married, but what was the harm in gazing at Steven for ten seconds too long? He would be confident, meeting my eyes and curling his lips, like he had bad intentions for him and me. Steven's attention made me aroused and uneasy, and I liked the feeling of both.

Shooting a movie far away from LA, especially in the sunshine, was like attending a sleepover or summer camp. We wound up in close quarters, the cast and crew, but—unlike sixth-grade Bible camp—no one was a virgin. Not even me.

A time zone away from home, it would be easy to slip up and pretend that I was accountable to no one. But—despite what they say—indiscretions do follow you home. More than that, the Almighty God was an ever-present force, watching over me. I felt I'd never spent a moment alone in my life. "What if Jesus walked in the room?" I heard Pastor Scott say while I gazed at Steven, heart aflutter.

⸺✦⸺

Staying with the director and two-thirds of the costume department wasn't as exhilarating as I'd imagined. My temporary housemates were under extreme stress because, on an indie budget, the cast and crew were spread thin.

As a purist (I believe that was the reason) Billy shot *Adventures in the Sin Bin* on film. With digital cameras you're welcome to shoot a million takes for the price of one, but on film, the team had three takes to nail it, max. After wrapping, Billy would pace around the house scratching his head, wishing there were more time between one day and the next.

Meanwhile, Marissa and Ellie shrank in size. Between scouring craft service for peanut butter cracker dinners and lugging the weight of a million clothes, the girls got slimmer. With twelve-to fourteen-hour relentless days, sleep was not on their horizon. They were so tired that when a friend gave us backstage, all-access passes to see Thom Yorke, the girls opted to plop on the couch. "I'd rather die," Ellie said.

Marissa flashed a tired smile. "I can't imagine standing up. Please go! Save yourself."

Shooting the film, I was on cloud nine, wanting the girls to fly up and meet me in heaven. "The set and the costumes—and the cast! Everything looks incredible." Whenever I was at the apartment I tried to bring the energy up, but it was impossible to alleviate their stress.

"Focus on your role," Marissa said. "Don't worry about us." Marissa was a tiny babe with chestnut locks and an array of bangles and bracelets that jingled when she walked. On set, she was a steady presence, quiet but brave. When I tried to help her carry shoes to the set, she said, "Get busy being a spoiled brat. We've got Atlas."

Our friend Atlas deserves more articulate descriptors than "amazing" or "incredible," but he really is amazing and incredible. Whenever I walked to wardrobe, he'd kiss my hand and dance us to the dressing room.

While I changed, Atlas averted his eyes and confessed the set's secrets. Atlas was an empath, able to intuit the interior lives of others. I found it inspiring that he'd never take ill behavior at face value. If an actor was angry or afraid, he saw the root cause, not the mere output of emotion. Atlas is a peel-back-the-curtain kind of person, and I loved him for it. I wondered whether he'd prove a safe place for me to try the truth on for size. But it didn't matter if I confessed. I was going to cheat on my husband, and Atlas knew it.

Because I recognized "sins" in the binary of black and white, I believed that good girls stayed married and bad girls got divorced. The latter category of women were forfeiting some piece of their soul. I should honor my vow, I thought, even if my callous attitude was bringing Brandon pain. I simply needed to work on diminishing my rage and we'd live happily ever after. Just give it time. Marriage made me feel miserable, betrayed, and sexually dissatisfied, but religious indoctrination told me there was no way out.

To be a good girl, I'd have to stay married, but, God, I wanted to leave. I'd make vague promises to Brandon, vacillating between staying and leaving, keeping him hostage in my emotional purgatory. My husband would grow weary and say, "We're together, right?" I promised we were but didn't know if my word meant anything anymore.

Emily cut her salmon with a fork and put it in her mouth. "That sounds awful," she said. Miles from LA, I was opening up to her, curious how my words might land on an unfamiliar soul. I reiterated my love for Jesus, not wanting to blow my destiny by admitting to misery. "So, did you even get married for love? Or just for sex?" There's a question you could ask a hundred evangelicals: How many of us confused a mutual sexual attraction for a happily ever after?

I told Emily the truth. "I got married because I felt guilty for having sex. I didn't want to stop hooking up, so I had to make it right."

"Can you see having kids with him?"

The thought made me cringe. Brandon and I fought endlessly over how I held brooms or how loudly I spoke. Some days I wasn't even sure he liked me. "Kids? No. Not with him."

"Not with him? Well, there's your answer."

But my "heart is deceitful." How could I really know?

The problem with my evangelical "good girl" persona is that

the less "good" I became, the less I perceived my actual sins. Remember, if true sin is the act of causing of harm, then it was wrong to string Brandon along, to force sexual situations and leave him in the dark. Our relationship was over, but I was scared to believe it. Being a good girl, worthy of heaven's gates, superseded my desire to leave. Meanwhile, my indecision was the sin, causing us both harm.

"But would you cheat on him?" Emily's asparagus-stabbed fork was suspended in the air.

I paused. "No."

Lovers, we don't always have the answer, but I'm telling you, this time I did.

Not physically drained like my hardworking wardrobe babes, Emily and I would run around Chicago at night. We'd grab dinner and drinks and share bottles of wine with our castmate Gabe. We spent hours at the museum, mocking modern art with Bo Burnham. The cast and crew became a little family—as they tend to do—and the filming itself was pure joy too.

For a real-life plot twist, my parents came to town. I love to travel with family, and seeing them would be like icing on the cake. They visited the set, and we stayed together at the cast's hotel. Ever nosy, Dad found the script and was horrified I'd have to simulate a blow job. Between his huffs and puffs, I begged him to understand. "It's a redemptive story!" I hadn't accepted the role casually. Jesus spoke in parables, and I believed certain stories needed to be told. *Sin Bin* wasn't a masterpiece of morality, but it was a human story about a girl—like me—trying her best while making a mini-disaster of her life.

Dad got over it and, between the love of my family and the buzz of the city, I forgot to worry about the marriage mess. With a lighter heart I sent Brandon pics of my costumes and one of me topless in the hotel mirror. To my horror, Brandon wrote back, "I can't wait to see you pregnant."

I deflated. This was not the erotic response I'd been hoping for.

Whenever I considered having Brandon's baby, I'd dream of myself in a white wire cage or in a house with the doors bolted shut. My psyche would scream, "You'd be trapped," but I kept up appearances. "That moment will be amazing," I messaged back.

I stepped into the tub—my favorite thinking place—and let the water kiss me all over. Showers mixed nicely with tears. It'd be easy to deny I'd been crying. Steam enveloped my face and offered a sense of privacy. In that solitude, I asked a question of the Divine. Will Brandon and I have kids?

No.

Call it a whisper from God or my own intuition. Either way, I knew. We weren't having kids.

But how could this be? I didn't want children tomorrow, but I wanted them someday. Did this imply Brandon would die? My "de-Nile" river ran deep enough that I presumed an untimely death over a divorce.

$\div$

Trusting oneself is crucial, and if what you've got faith in is bursting forth from a place of conviction, then I trust you too. But a lot of us are lying when we say what we desire. We lie and lie and lie, hoping our hearts will catch up to our mouths.

For example, as a teen I said, "I want to sleep with one man for the rest of my life."

Did I come to this "desire" on my own?

Nope.

If I said what I meant, I'd have said, "Pastor Scott taught me that God created marriage between a man and a woman. When you're married you can have sex. If you're not married but have sex, you risk eternal damnation. If I choose to sleep with someone outside of marriage, it will have been a selfish, lustful act that dishonors my future husband. My body will be less than, having lost irretrievable pieces, like a broken chocolate bar. I'll be gross, like chewed up gum. Worst of all, I won't be a good Christian. This is why I won't be having sex out of wedlock."

Romantic, I know.

When Steven climbed on top of me, I knew that having sex with more than one person was something I'd always wanted. Purity called me names like selfish, evil, and perverse, but this was my desire. The weight of his body comforted me.

Here is how the affair started. One night, after wrap, an actor we'll call Jason invited a group of us to his hotel room. Mom and Dad were gone by now, so I wanted to be in the presence of the cast day and night. Summer camp was coming to an end, and my heart grew sick imagining that finality.

Up in Jason's room, we popped champagne and sat wherever, on the bed and at the tables. We played music and yelled jokes, vying for the room's attention.

By then, I'd had many periods. Despite the challenge of dealing with gushing blood, I was a seasoned vet. Sure, on rare occasions there'd be a spill, but for the most part I changed my tampons in the nick of time. But not tonight.

I was blabbing a mimosa-induced story to Atlas when I felt the wet. Blood had run through my underwear. I prayed the crimson wave hadn't made its way through my skirt.

I did a check, on the sly, and plopped back down. Oh shit. On Jason's white, fluffy bed was a pool of cherry red. "Oh my God," I said. And don't accuse me of taking the Lord's name in vain; I was literally praying.

"What?" I looked up and there stood Steven, digging his hands in his pockets.

"Huh?"

CHAPTER II

"'Oh my God,' what?"

Atlas returned from the bathroom and they stood there together, hovering above me. The moment called for standing up, but I maintained my position. "How are you, gentlemen?"

Atlas squinted at me, searching for the source of my awkwardness. He was a powerful soothsayer or psychic, but he couldn't intuit my bloody predicament.

Steven kicked his boots and looked down at me. "I'm fine. It's been a long day."

"I'm sad it's almost over."

"I'll miss you," Steven said. Atlas flashed me an exaggerated eye roll and sat elsewhere, with Emily.

Mind you, my head was spinning. Steven could've asked for my number or for the time and I would have nodded, stupefied. I was on autopilot, thinking blood, blood, blood! Finally, "Could you bring me some wine?"

Steven perked up. "Of course," and left for the minibar.

I watched him grab a glass and pour a cheap pinot noir. "There you go."

I needed more time. "Could you bring me a napkin too?"

Steven looked perplexed, but he obliged. I said "napkin" because I didn't see any. I needed him lost and distracted for as long as possible.

With Steven gone, I lifted my butt into the air and dumped the entire glass of wine on the bed. I slid forward, glanced back and— boom—I had nailed it. Red on red—there was no difference in hue. Satisfied, I stood and tied a jacket around my waist. I made a sound like, "Oh," to draw some attention. Jason noticed his drenched bed. "Oh shit."

"I'm sorry, babe. I'm such a klutz."

"You need another?" Steven was in front of me now, close to my face. Air released from my lungs and his words hung in the air, begging for an answer.

Taking a cue from the good girl I aspired to be, I said, "I should head back."

"I'll walk you," he offered.

"To Billy's?"

"To wherever." He scanned the room, with discretion. "To my room?"

My heart stopped. Steven maintained his gaze while our bodies drew closer, unable to resist the energetic pull. Steven smelled like the boys I loved in high school, slathered in mall-bought cologne. His breath, I imagined, would taste like salty sweat and wheat.

"Okay."

"Yeah?" He put down his beer and slapped his hands together. "How do we do this? With nobody noticing?"

I bit my cheek and shrugged. I'd heard he was in an open relationship. I didn't think that dynamic was real, assuming whoever used the label "open" was simply looking to cheat. Maybe his relationship status was a lie, maybe he was telling the truth. Either way, I was locked in, my body vibrating at the possibility of his touch.

"#305. In ten?" Steven left to get a head start.

Meanwhile, I bid farewell to the room, pretending to be sleepy. I was giving the best performance of the week, acting like I wasn't covered in blood, acting like I wasn't going to cheat.

"I'm tired too," Atlas said. "Let's go, baby." In the elevator he asked, "Shall we split a cab?"

I gave Atlas a sheepish grin. Atlas is spiritually attuned. There was no hiding from him. "I'm not gonna do anything."

He squinted, like my lies were blinding.

"You're married, Brenda. I mean, fuck who you want and be single, but don't cheat. It's immoral." We stepped off the elevator and the doors shut. "Honey, you want to fuck Steven."

"Not really—"

"We all want to fuck Steven, okay?"

A knee-jerk reaction told me to protest, to continue denying the truth, but I was exhausted. Between propping up my marriage on its shattered foundation and longing for retaliation, I lost the will to fight.

"Then, call him," Atlas said. Atlas tried to teach me about honesty and integrity. "Say, Brandon, I love you but it's over." Then he grabbed my hands. "Brenda, if you walk upstairs after that, you can hold your head high. If you break up with him, you did the right thing."

This advice did not reside in black and white. In the grey, Atlas didn't guilt me for a potential divorce or for having impure thoughts. Atlas was merely inviting me to a new sexual ethic, one I was not ready to embrace.

"I'm gonna go up."

He frowned. "I'll see your dumb ass tomorrow." We did a double cheek kiss, and I headed back to the elevator.

I ascended to the third floor and knocked on #305. Steven opened the door, like he'd been waiting. "I thought Atlas apprehended you." He motioned to the bed. "You want a drink?"

"Tequila?"

"Sure."

"Could I borrow a shirt?" Though I'd been doused in blood and pinot, when I cleaned up and returned from the bathroom Steven said he couldn't care less. He leaned in for a kiss. I grabbed the back of his head and pulled him in closer. We'd been building up to this affair, but I couldn't believe it was happening.

Purity god was a companion I trusted for half my life. Now, in a flash, he'd abandoned me. He'd provided neither education nor integrity to empower me. Purity told me because of the sex party, my flirting, and these kisses, I'd be lukewarm, spit out of God's mouth. Sitting there, I decided, I'm garbage. I will burn. I drank to oblivion because God was gonna hate me anyway. Then Steven and I had sex.

Our little love affair could only carry on a few more days. People said I smelled like him, that mall-bought cologne seeping into my skin. Steven's scent was distinct, and I wore it like a scarlet letter.

Atlas said that people were calling me a cheater. When Emily asked, I denied it. I hated to be a liar, afraid to get caught, but on the day I flew back to LA, I realized that I didn't care what happened.

If Billy or Ellie had caught me in a lie, so be it. If Brandon dumped me, he'd have done what I was not brave enough to do. "Set me free, Brandon," I thought. I wanted my husband to unlock the white wire cage and release me.

After landing at LAX, I hopped the shuttle to Penn Station. I talked a big game on the plane but now I was worried again about getting caught. I felt like a sham.

Brandon swooped me up in his yellow bug and threw my luggage in the trunk. We exchanged stories, but the mood was tense. I'd grown colder and more distant each time I tumbled into Steven's bed. I blamed Brandon for pushing me into this infidelity. I resented Steven for letting me seduce him. When Brandon carried my bags up the stairs to our apartment, I heard him whimper. I was sad to be home and he knew it.

Inside, I settled onto our velvet couch and popped a yogurt. Brandon took a seat on the couch too. He sat as far away as possible, and I froze. This is it.

"You smell like a man."

In a moment like this, the brain presents several options. There's the truth, which is often bumped to the bottom of the list. Then there's excuse after excuse. I thought of dumb lies, about switching my perfume or how Billy's house stank like an Abercrombie and Finch, but instead I chose silence.

Brandon moved to the edge of his seat and tipped his hat. Ask me, I thought. I hate you, so, ask me. I'm ready, bitch.

"What do you want for dinner?"

Oof. Secrecy was his decision. I cheated and Brandon knew, but my husband decided we would continue hiding from one another.

A few weeks later, I cleared out my closet, feigning a spring cleaning. I yanked the yellow tags of the trashbags I'd be donating to Goodwill and lugged them to the car. "You're moving out," he said.

"No, I'm not," I protested, but this was another lie.

12

JEZEBEL

We were in a pretty one bedroom in the heart of Silver Lake. There was a picture window that looked out over the hills. We were perched above Sunset Boulevard, in the trees, like two little birds, Chelsea and me. I call Chelsea "Tiny" because she's oh-so-petite. We carried clothes and treasures into our sweet little home, convinced that living together would become a grand adventure. In those days we were single and free.

At least, I wanted to be free.

My religion spoke of "freedom in Christ," but that concept had been aligned with purity culture. Purity said that my "freedom" would be the supernatural ability to flee from sexual sin, meaning premarital sex or homosexuality. We were free, free, free, to be the pastor's narrow interpretation of what the Bible told us to be.

When we were preteens, Pastor Scott urged us to shackle our hormones, and Purity god turned the key. With your inherent, God-given sexuality demonized—quite literally—you imagined your sexuality a beast, salivating at the chance to destroy your walk with God. Ergo, the beast had overtaken Brandon and—shortly after—me. Church would say we'd fallen prey to our wicked desires but that—good news—Christ could set us free. God offers a supernatural power, they said, to tame our wicked sexuality.

Achieving this "freedom in Christ" meant you would solely desire your husband or wife. This power could free you from porn addiction. If this hormonal beast—which is in cahoots with the devil—made you lust for the "wrong" gender, this "freedom" could flip your desire. With enough prayer and petition, you'll want the "right" sex, you'll see. This is why the "same-sex attracted" or "ex-gays"—as they're often referred to in church—would claim to be "free" from the sin of homosexuality.

The phrase "freedom in Christ" became shorthand for navigating a "biblical" sex life, even if this "freedom" strangled your spirit to death.

When I moved in with Chelsea, I had this script in my mind. "There is freedom in Christ." To achieve this, "I must flee sexual immorality."

I hung photos in our living room and swept up the dust we'd dragged in. Chelsea, in her tiny jeans and her tiny top, breezed through the living room and flashed a huge smile. Our place was quaint, but we had what we needed. One bathroom with a high-pressure shower, hardwood floors throughout, and a bit of privacy provided by the surrounding trees. We could sunbathe on the patch of grass we called our front yard. Tiny and I stocked the teal-and-black-tiled kitchen with pot stickers, tandoori, and a case of Two Buck Chuck from Trader Joe's. I brought a couple of beers into the living room and joined Tiny on the couch. "So, what are you gonna do," she asked, "start dating?"

Purity is famous for his slogans, like, "It's Adam and Eve, not Adam and Steve!" "Pray the gay away!" And of course, the horrific "God hates fags!" Purity god and Satan love that shit. Anything that alienates LGBTQ+ people from the love of Jesus is a win for evil. However, as a straight-leaning, non-virgin woman, I didn't find Purity's sayings applicable anymore. Purity demanded that I—as a divorcee—return to being sexless in body and mind. But I hadn't been sexless to begin with. I was born with sexuality and sensuality, these elements of me dancing together, intermingling, and leading to what I once saw as evil. Shame pursued me. The Antagonist called me unholy and bad. 2 Corinthians 7:1: "Let us purify ourselves from everything that contaminates body and spirit, perfecting holiness out of reverence for God." Purity accused me of denying God's Word. I must abstain, refrain, purify my mind and—

Snap! Swish! The pendulum went swinging. "Of course I want to date," I said. "I'm excited." And with that I took a hefty swig of beer.

Religion held me—unnaturally so—at the top of a pendulum's swing. I was meant to be perfect, blameless, and chaste. Virginity made me a "real Christian," and though that defining feature was gone, Purity still held me up there, bound with a flimsy string of cherry-picked Bible verses. As excited as I was to be living in this pretty little house with my dearest best friend, life would be agony until . . . swish! I felt freedom—for real—for the first time.

I bade farewell to chastity and climbed out from beneath the steeple. I became like the prodigal son, walking away from his father. "I'll come back, if You'll have me," I prayed. I thought I was losing the love of my life.

On the way out, Purity warned that I might die in a fluke accident, and that if I did I would be sent to hell for eternity. But Purity also said that to have God I must abandon sex. Therefore, to have sex and explore, I'd have to abandon God. "Please forgive me, Jesus," I begged. "Don't leave me."

Tiny, my new housemate, was born and raised in LA. She's one of four girls, and in their household sex talk wasn't taboo. Her mom was a liberal babe who lost her virginity to an iconic '80s heartthrob, who shall remain unnamed.

Living with a non-Christian meant I could avoid stressful conversations. If I slept elsewhere, Chelsea wouldn't blink an eye, let alone fold her arms and demand, "Where were you?" Instead, we could sit on the edge of her bed and rehash the details. I wanted to share bowls of Neapolitan ice-cream as though life were a sleepover and talk about boys, boys, boys.

However, my prodigal son journey was not inspired by sexual desire alone. In fact, when I moved in with Tiny, I didn't want sex. Brandon and Steven were in my rearview mirror, and I wanted to navigate this portion of the journey without them. Sexual experience was a motivator, sure, but the fruit of awareness was what I craved. This hunger for knowledge made me empathize with mother Eve.

Eve, I realized, resided in a black-and-white garden where good and evil drew clear lines. Without pain, without shame, Eve and Adam were in paradise. The couple basked in their utopia, eating off the land and tumbling through the grass, stark naked.

In the midst of the lovebirds' bliss, our Creator kept one tree off limits: the tree of knowledge, and Eve couldn't resist. With the snake slithering up her arm, she took a bite. Eve wanted to know something, I supposed. Perhaps she wanted to know everything.

Pastor Everyman vilifies mother Eve. They say she was not flawed but evil, ushering humanity into our original sin. "The world could have been perfect," they say, "if not for Eve." But if Eden was such a paradise, why did Eve risk losing her home?

Sex was my forbidden fruit, dangling from the tree of knowledge. Promiscuous sex—like life—is agony, ecstasy, and the gamut of emotions in between. Sex offers knowledge, and that knowledge was what I wanted.

As the story goes, Eve bit the apple and brought death to this earth, but I've been taught that life is temporal and God's love is eternal. What if she understood that true love requires choice and that to know pleasure she must experience pain? What if the agony of childbirth was a blessing and not a curse, the depth of pain being what brings forth life? If knowing begets beauty, perhaps a bite of the apple made her brave, not evil.

Then, as a sweet companion would, she'd ask Adam if he wanted a bite.

❧

Tiny and I plopped on our cushy couch and settled in for a movie. "I'm not gonna count," I said. Our extended sleepover began, over sweet potato fries and chocolate chip cookies.

"Oh really?" Tiny would raise and extend the "llllly" like a proper valley girl. "Why not?"

To have sex unencumbered—not weighted by the world of evangelicalism or by the societal expectations put on women—I wouldn't tally my exploits. "Because sex should be a moment in time, not a number. If I hit five, six, seven people I'll force myself to stop, and I'm tired of all that. I can't count." I was spontaneous but not accustomed to free rein. In the pursuit of sex, I hoped to find myself by ditching Purity altogether. I didn't have the term "deconstruction," so I called this my prodigal journey.

I thought—as I'd been told of Eve's—that my pursuit of this knowledge would be selfish and destructive. And though sex without integrity can be both of those things, the root of my desire was not selfish. I wanted to know God—the real one. I suspected that I'd been duped by Purity, but I couldn't prove it. Prodigal life would deconstruct what I once believed and—again, like Eve—I was willing to risk my afterlife to find the truth.

The pendulum swung. I ripped down the apple and took a mighty bite.

On my way out of Eden—bags packed and U-Haul boxes strewn across the lawn—I thought God had let me go. But really, He moved with us into the pretty place perched above Sunset Boulevard. God—the real one—wouldn't ditch His girl, whether or not I perceived His presence.

❧

This grey world is made from polarities of light and darkness. The purest of good draws the cruelest of evil because the opposing polarities recognize one another. Evil taints good but light shines on darkness because God allows both. Having been granted free will, we celebrate and suffer as citizens of this planet.

With sex mirroring divine love, sex done in divinity has the power to heal and unify. While making love—for goodness' sake—life itself can burst into existence. God is Creator, and with sex we mirror him, becoming creators ourselves.

I'd been told that evil sex is sexuality outside of marriage or sex that I'd dare have with another woman. I can promise you, we got this wrong.

Freedom is not achieved by shackling one's hormones and crying after one has masturbated in the shower. Enthusiastic consent is not present between the man and woman whose orientations repel each other, like two negative poles on magnets. Mutuality cannot exist when a wife is strong-armed—by Bible verses—into submission. None of this is God-honoring sex, but at the time of this chapter, I thought it was.

Ironically, by teaching our Christian teens purity over integrity, we empower evil sex to win. The most evil sex is when a child is raped by a pastor or priest who says her spaghetti-strapped Jezebel spirit made him do it, citing Romans 14:13, which commands "that no man put a stumbling block or an occasion to fall in his brother's way." This is an extreme example, but it's occurred often enough to become a cliché. That's a fact that should horrify Christians. The church's rape culture is downright evil.

But if we're talking about evil sex, examples needn't be that extreme. There is a myriad of grey to contend with in sexuality.

For example, many women realized—in the wake of #MeToo—that we've been kinda, maybe raped a little, we think?

I am one of those women. Purity had given me the word "No" until I wore a white dress. I wasn't given language like, "That hurts" or "I've changed my mind," which left an abysmal gap in my sexual understanding.

Ignorance, lovers, is not bliss when it comes to sex. This is why parents need to advocate for comprehensive, age-appropriate sex education. A three-year-old deserves to know that her body has sexual organs and that they belong to her alone. If we hide the fact that our bodies were made for pleasure, children may not understand that it's wrong when those body parts are in pain. A teenager needs to become aware of the clitoris and that it's for the enjoyment of her sexuality. She deserves to know that if someone touches her and it hurts or it's scary, then something is amiss. No matter what age or gender, children ought to be taught that our body is not to be touched without our permission. If we allow children to politely decline hugs, they're better equipped to recognize personal agency and consent. A rich, comprehensive sex education—rather than "abstinence only"—empowers students with the phrase, "I don't want to be here." Or, "I want to be here, but let's not have sex like that." Mothers and fathers, I beg you to be less concerned with your daughter's consensual sex life and more concerned that she'll have drunk sex at a party, sans condom, because she didn't want to "premeditate sin." After all, abstinence-only sex ed—even among Christians—has been shown to delay sexual activity by only several months on average. Purity rings, chastity balls, and even guilt and shame aren't as successful as we think.

I am horrified to realize how little I knew about mutuality and consent when I needed it the most. And you can judge me all you want for being a Jezebel, tumbling through the bar scene looking for sex, but this is a twenty-some-year-old girl we're talking about. Maybe this blondie should have known better, but she'd married young. She'd devoted herself to one man. She'd saved herself for marriage (almost) and was betrayed by cheating. Freshly divorced Brenda was a misguided but well-intentioned babe with a broken heart. Her church—which she thought was her god—promised her a happily ever after, and it had all fallen apart.

A girl like that, gallivanting about LA, Christian or otherwise, deserves to not be raped or mistreated. She deserves to know a man has no right to film her naked, without her consent. Our daughters and sons deserve better than not to know their worth.

My situation is unique in that I was indoctrinated not by my family but by the evangelical church. My household was sex-silent but not sex-negative. Still, we had no language to protect ourselves. Mom told me I could call her—no questions asked—if I were in a predicament that required a ride home. "You won't be grounded," she promised. "Just tell me you're in trouble." This is wonderful, but when our kids become adults and move three thousand miles away, they're forced to get themselves out of sticky situations. Or to lie back and hope it'll be over soon.

My #MeToo moment was confusing because I hadn't verbalized a no. My body language said no, my eyes pleaded that he stop, but when he left I didn't tell a soul. I believed it happened because I'd become gross and slutty enough to sleep with someone I wasn't attracted to. In the aftermath, the disgust was toward myself, believing the assault to be a sign that my morality had tanked. In fact, I didn't recognize it as an assault at all. Nonconsensual sex was supposed to take place in dark alleys or with your hands pinned above your head. Violence would be involved, which is the proof you'd been violated. I'd carry a black canister of mace and be on guard. I'd be strong and tough. Sexual violence would be easy to spot. Good and smart women knew how to avoid an assault.

Thus began the season I refer to as my trampage. I intend this as a term of endearment because it was a euphoric and expansive time. To rid of myself of Purity's repressive constraints, I behaved as I wanted. But because sex is powerful and experiences of it can range from darkness to light, I experienced a gamut of things. My trampage brought agony and ecstasy to my very soul.

Let's begin on the brighter end of the spectrum, with Davey. Yup, the one that Sienna said had "a perfect dick."

Tiny and I attended a birthday party. Upon our arrival, I saw Davey with his feet dangling over the pool. He'd been mid-conversation, but he excused himself, rolled down his pant cuffs, and strolled right over.

Throughout the party, we did the dance, clocking each other's moves and searching eyes for desire. He didn't expect I'd be willing to go home, since I was such a "good girl," so we remained in a holding pattern, not kissing, not touching, at the party till the sun came up.

By now, Tiny had bid us farewell. Others went to bed. I wondered, "God, is he ever going to make a move?" Davey finally asked, "Would you like to go somewhere with me?" We took his olive-green Jaguar to the Café 101 in Beachwood. We shared a stack of pancakes and traded strawberry and vanilla milkshakes until our eyes drooped with sleep. "Do you want to come home with me?"

I bit the straw and smiled. "At last."

Davey's place was in Hollywood proper, close enough to the Chinese Theatre that you could find it by following the pavement's trail of stars. Davey lived in darkness, like a vampire. The place was furnished with rich wood and red velvet. He pulled thick curtains over the windows and headed for the record player. I sat on his bed. "How can you sleep on this? It's like a rock."

"I love a hard bed. I can't sleep in chicks' beds." Davey placed the needle on a Rolling Stones record and sighed. "Like, this one woman I'm fucking, she gets upset when I leave but she has too many pillows. I mean, her bed's too soft." Davey spoke like this, cavalier regarding his exploits. After the dishonesty of my past relationships, this candor was refreshing. I poked and prodded about what else he might be up to, and Davey said, "Look, we're having fun, right? I'm in love with my ex, and you just got a divorce."

"Right." I was nervous about falling hard or being hurt again, but what he said made sense.

"Are you looking for a boyfriend?"

"Not really."

"And if you were looking," Davey spun around and shot me finger guns, "would you pick me?"

I laughed, "God, no," and leaned in for our first kiss.

Davey was the first of many things. He was my first casual sex partner and the first man who never hurt me. We were two people, young, uninvolved, and sexually charged. Our dynamic worked. Davey took me to dinner, laughed at my stories, and cared in a way that was both romantic and blasé. We tumbled into bed, on and off, for a year a half. When he whined about his ex, my heart never hurt. I hoped he could win her back.

Having practiced a relationship that was both casual and erotic, I met John at a friend's loft. By then, I was deep into operation trampage, with my seductive powers honed in. When John massaged and caressed me, I was at maximum Jezebel, taking him in. The sex was enthusiastic indeed, and John, like Davey, pursued more than my body. Our relationship was unattached, but the term "casual" never implied a lack of intimacy.

Purity culture told me I'd go crawling on my knees, begging for forgiveness and ashamed of my sexual choices, but I wasn't experiencing that sort of condemnation at all. Sure, I had to navigate sensitive reactions to "casual" intimacy. Casual is hardly ever that. But I'd be lying if I said the whole trampage was a mess. I learned about myself in the beds of John and Davey. I found it impossible to regret those moments. These men explored my propensity for pleasure with tenderness and care. They considered my emotions with utmost clarity and support. We weren't making love in the truest sense of the term, but these were experiences of enthusiastic consent and mutuality.

※

Evangelicalism did not properly identify ungodly sex. The questions Purity posed were:

1. Are you married?
2. Are you married to a person of the opposite sex?
3. Are you giving your body to the man you married? Or, Are you doing enough to be worthy of the sex you're requesting from your wife?

If you could answer yes to these three questions, you were honoring God with your sexuality. Purveyors of purity culture pretended that godly sex was that simple. The nuance or complication in straying from these rules was ignored or spoken away. Instead of assessing the grey areas of sexuality, Purity taught from a place of fear.

If we tell kids about anal, they'll want to try it.

If we remove the stigma from buying condoms, the kids will buy them.

If we allow our daughters to use birth control, they'll become promiscuous.

Christians tend to fear sex education, but information is empowering. In places like Texas, where sex education is limited, abortions and teen pregnancy rates remain high. The Netherlands and California, however, offer comprehensive sex education, and the proof is in their fruit. With comprehensive, fact-based sex education, abortion and teen pregnancy rates fall.

Empowering the children we love with education is a sacred gift. I know it's difficult to give a gift you were not given yourself. I have compassion for parents who are bogged down by their own shame, their trauma, and what they perceive to be their mistakes. But when our response is to rant and rave about hookup culture and keep our kids under lock and key, we are not protecting them but delaying the inevitable. Without education, without the belief that they deserve autonomy and pleasure, the inevitable may be sex that is unenjoyable or, worse yet, traumatic. A woman may bleed during intercourse because she and her partner weren't taught about lubricant. A wife may endure vaginismus, having internalized sexual guilt. Or, with Guttmacher Institute reporting that 54 percent of abortion clients identified as Christian in 2014, your son or daughter might have an abortion in the dark, terrified of what you'll say.

Parents, don't allow these points to invite you into deeper sexual shame. Few people I know were raised with sex positivity. It's no wonder we've struggled to cultivate that communication ourselves. However, Jesus spoke in parables, and we've lived stories of our own. If your teens shrink in their seats, begging you to spare the details, don't gross them out but stay the course and share your story. When there's a question about sex, next time they'll know whom to ask if you're the open book.

Sex is complicated. Purity, with his fear mongering and shame, can make sex a god-awful thing. If we heed the voice of The Antagonist, sex can become a point of contention and a source of pain for our entire dang life.

What did this look like for me?

Now that I wasn't married, Purity's three-point list proved wildly insufficient. According to Purity, I was outside of God's favor and therefore on my own. When I had sex, I asked Jesus to wait outside. Pastors said, "Don't do anything you'd be afraid of Jesus seeing," so I was left fending for dignity in those rooms all alone.

Most often, I was fine. I'd have dissatisfying or disconnected sex but tolerate the experience for an orgasm or a good story. Other times, I'd wish things had gone differently. I had sex with people I didn't want to have sex with.

Women are often scoffed at and blamed for this sort of compliance. Having sex without wanting to is incomprehensible to people if they haven't been there themselves. Christians say, "This is why you need to be married," or, "Hello, you should have just left." The Antagonist's greatest feat is to convince a victim their assault was a fault of their own. "She shouldn't have been there in the first place," someone vomits on Twitter. These things aren't said to our face as often as they're hollered by pundits on TV. These messages are insidious, and they stick. Little boys and girls are listening.

Jodie Foster's portrayal of a rape victim in *The Accused* was revolutionary for its time because it begged the audience to view assault from a nuanced lens. The courts—for decades—said a claim of rape wasn't valid if it was the fault of what the victim wore or didn't say. "Was there a verbal no?" Jodie's character had implied a no but hadn't said it, forcibly splayed on the bar's pinball machine and taken over by a group of men. I saw this movie as a girl and remembered the court noted that she'd been dancing, that she consented to kisses. In many cases, flirtatious behavior nullified a person's right to claim rape. Nowadays, high-profile dismissals continue to occur, but with our collective conscious evolving, a judge is no longer permitted to ask, "What were you wearing?" They'll ask instead, "Did you verbalize a no?" Drug or alcohol consumption can still negate a victim's story altogether.

I hadn't recognized my rape until the advent of #MeToo. Writing "rape" feels counterintuitive still, my bias believing that rape requires violence and restraint.

A "kinda, sorta, maybe, was that rape?" rape happened to me on a vacation. A dear friend invited me to accompany her, her husband, and several friends to a luxury hotel in Aspen. Money was my main impediment. "I can't afford that, babe. I'm sorry."

"You won't pay for a thing," my girlfriend explained. Their friend was one of the wealthiest men in her hometown, with an armored car and full staff. "If he dropped a hundred-dollar bill, it wouldn't be worth his time to pick it up," she said.

Regardless of the fact that my suite, private ski lessons, and decadent meals would be a drop in the bucket, I was not quick to trust the arrangement. As they say, nothing is for free.

"I promise," she said. "I talked to him. He understands. You're not obligated to anything. He just offered that I bring a friend."

Had I not been compartmentalized, with Purity dividing my

spirit from my body, my flesh from the Divine, I might have recognized the sinking in my belly. When I imagined the trip, I received a Ping! Like, "Beware!" I was accustomed to anxiety, however, experiencing the steady hum of "something amiss" since I'd been introduced to Purity.

I believed everything I did was a sin, so I ignored the warning and packed for the trip.

Skiing was the worst. I'd tumble down the mountain at eight miles per hour and sink into the snow. I'd beg the sun to set already, to please release me from this recreational hell. I wanted to sip hot toddies from the hotel bar. But my host, Silvio, had been generous. Skiing wasn't pleasant, but I fell down that hill every dang day to be the embodiment of his money well spent.

In the evenings, Silvio ordered sushi, sashimi, and ugami. Shame enveloped me like a cloud when the men pulled out their credit cards to pay. Money, clothing, or food in exchange for affection is a common arrangement between older, richer men and pretty, young women. Though it was communicated that I wouldn't be required to earn my keep, I'd climb into the plush hotel bed wracked with guilt. What did I do to deserve this luxury?

Integrity would have taught that I'm inherently valuable, and not at all like chewed gum. Integrity suggests we speak directly and openly. By that measure, I should have rested in the fact that my intentions had been clearly communicated. This trip was a gift, we'd decided, and Silvio was to require nothing of me.

My friend and I spent three days skiing, dining, and drinking. In my friend's hotel room, Silvio clinked my glass and wrapped his arm around my waist. He had kept a respectful distance, but now, on our last night, he was rubbing my thighs, closing in. I avoided his kiss with a turn of my head. Fear bubbled in my gut while I looked at his bloated face. I'd been stupid enough to accept a "free" trip.

Silvio's and my pheromones were oil and vinegar—there was no unity or substance between us. I had made him laugh, but otherwise we'd barely spoken. I appreciated his generosity and told him so, before excusing myself and going to bed.

I'd been lying there for hours, sound asleep, when I heard a click. The door of my hotel room was swinging open, slowly.

My instinct was to bolt up in bed or to call his name. I could say, "Silvio," in a tone a mother might use to chastise her child. Silvio was doing something wrong, and I wanted him to know it. More importantly, I wanted him to leave.

Like an animal in danger, I lay there frozen, hoping my stillness would send the predator away. "He must know I'm sleeping," I thought. I held my arms to my chest but kicked my legs out, silently, to take up more space on the bed. The plan was to remain motionless and to be impossible to rouse.

Then he turned on the light. Silvio lifted the blanket and moved my legs aside, so he could lie beside me.

My plan had gotten shaky. I didn't dream he'd fling on the light or enter my space without warning. While I pretended to sleep, his hands moved to pull down my underwear. I heard him unwrap a condom, I watched him climb on top of me, and I waited for it to be over. Afterward he kissed my mouth, acknowledging me. "So good," he said, as though I'd been a willing participant.

When he left, I couldn't sleep so I washed off. Might as well enjoy the bath, I thought. "You certainly earned it." I poured a glass of wine and ate Oreos in the tub, trying to make sense of what happened. Not understanding that wrong had been done to me, I spiraled into shame.

The Antagonist licked its lips, salivating over a moment like this. "You've gotten real slutty, haven't you? You didn't even like him." I got a flash of his fat tummy resting on mine, and it made me ill.

I'm a full-blown slut, I decided. I couldn't believe I'd stooped so low. Carelessly banging band members was one thing but sleeping with a repulsive dude for a free trip? Wow, Brenda. You've really lost your dignity.

I never told my girlfriend what happened. "Did you fuck Silvio?" she asked me playfully the next day.

"God no," I said.

Her face clocked confusion. "Oh. I thought that you did." Silvio told her we had sex. She must've wondered who was lying.

At breakfast, he hugged me cheerfully and kissed me on the cheek. Integrity would have screamed, "She didn't make eye contact, dumbass. She didn't want you, and you didn't ask."

Purity whispered, "That's what you get."

I'm over the moon that Americans are catching up to the truth: The green light to sexual activity is an enthusiastic yes, not the mere absence of a no. But after this maybe/sort of/was that rape, I grew more flippant about sex. The Aspen situation symbolized—to me—a lack of value for my sexuality. After the rape, sharing my body more freely seemed appropriate and just the same. I'd have a few more instances of not knowing how to leave or accepting sex because someone made me feel badly for not saying yes. Entertaining these memories nauseates me. But writing my experience is worthwhile because, between #MeToo and #ChurchToo, I know I'm not alone.

I'll warn you that, from here on, the book gets a great deal sadder. I dread reliving certain events for the sake of putting them on paper, but again, it'll be worth it. Although this story is my own, the emotions, the shame, the humanity in me are universal. Psalm 147:3 says: "He heals the brokenhearted and binds up their wounds."

Sexual assault wounds the soul. Compounding that assault with shame invites the wounding to continue. It is not victim-blaming to say that those of us harmed by sex can have a difficult time staying away from harm in the future. We cannot always protect ourselves from predators, but if we believe we deserved an assault or that it was our fault, it's difficult to recognize when it's happening again.

Then there are moments of consent that are still difficult to navigate because you want it, but you don't want it *like that*. Purity offered no language to help us advocate for ourselves in these situations, even when our partner would be happy to oblige.

In New York City's Soho House, Emily and Georgie had my hair teased up like Dolly Parton's. I modeled for Pretty Pony's presentation, and after the show I met a man at Blind Barber. I was being my usual minxy self, ordering a dirty martini with extra olives. "Extra dirty." He and I laughed together at the absurdity of a joke so cheesy. I wrote my number on a napkin and cabbed to his place, because I wanted to.

The guy was shaggy and sexy, and I was trampaging (always, always, always with a condom by the way). I imagined that a man like him, with a puppy-dog grin, would wind up in the stack of my positive sexual experiences. He'd be horrified to know otherwise, because he is a good person. I should know; we stayed friends.

Without integrity's language of, "That hurts. Let's have sex a different way," I went into shock when he got aggressive. We were having sex in a way that I'd enjoy with a partner, with someone I trusted. But because I didn't know him and because I fancied my body less than precious, I had my first out-of-body experience. I floated outside myself and hovered above. I watched him choking me and yanking my head back, and I thought, "This is what happens when you have unmarried sex. Sometimes it goes well, and other times you get what you deserve."

I wasn't present in my body. Therefore, I was powerless to stop and change course. I watched this guy hurt me, a guy who would've been happy to do things in a way that I preferred. In this case, the problem was not exclusively in what he did but in what I could not say.

The last thing I'll tell you about sex on the worse end of the spectrum is something that I've never shared. This was a secret I wished to keep forever because—to me—this was the proof that I'd become truly worthless. I still thought that one day I'd remedy my ways. I'd be a good mom, of course. But the chance of a good man loving me was decreasing. If I were a candy bar, like Pastor Scott said, my last piece of chocolate had melted, forgotten in somebody's back pocket.

Home alone and fresh out of the shower, I reached inside myself and found a used condom.

Nowadays, I know this can happen. Sex can be messy and funny and make embarrassing sounds. You may even lose a condom somehow. The night before had been drunken but consensual. In a calmer state, I might have gone straight to the pharmacy for a Plan B. But instead, I lost control and wept on the bedroom floor, certain I was dirty and worthless.

In truth, the stray condom hadn't made me less of a woman. The incident, however, did symbolize a disconnect between myself and my body. This condom was more than safe sex gone awry. Every time I asked God to "wait outside" of my sexual experiences, I became further compartmentalized, body from spirit from mind.

SUCCUBUS

Whenever I missed God, I'd bike to church. I'd throw my unkempt hair into a bun and press a skater helmet on top. I'd fly down Sunset Boulevard, past the yoga studio, past the latex sex shop. I'd whisk around the middle school, which on Sundays became the venue for Mosaic Church.

Dishonoring my body, believing spirit to be holy and flesh to be evil, I chastised her—my body—when she acted up. While dismounting and locking my bike, my arms would shake. "Pull it together, Bren." I clapped my hands against my thighs to gain bearing. My fingers trembled, which made it difficult to secure the padlock. Church congregants shook hands in the sunlight. Girls flocked the coffee stand like a gaggle of geese, happy, happy, happy, pouring their free coffees and adding vanilla cream. I juggled an Oaks latte all the way down from Franklin Boulevard to avoid this small talk, but a parishioner approached me nonetheless.

With the fear I felt, you'd think this woman was wearing a white mask and holding a butcher's knife, like Michael Meyers. I reeled back like she could knock me over the head with her NIV Bible. "Run," my body said, "Run!"

I chastised and teased my body. I told her she was being ridiculous. Look at this sweet woman in her ponytail and yellow top. "She's harmless," I promised. I crossed my arms to stop the shuddering.

Not until reading Jamie Lee Finch's book *You Are Your Own* did

I recognize that my body had been protecting me. The nice lady brandished no weaponry, but I was in danger nonetheless. Our body keeps account of offenses, even when we've forgiven them, and especially if we've forgotten.

At church, I would be exposed to the booming voices of Purity and his best friend The Antagonist. The worship songs would affirm that I had no inherent value in the absence of Jesus. "I don't deserve it and still you give yourself away." I was there to worship God, the way I had as a child, but these lyrics were too cruel for my body. "These songs have been hurting you," she said.

I forced a smile at the yellow-topped woman heading in my direction.

"Do you have a small group?"

I cringed. "Not currently." I wanted to visit church, but I wasn't ready to engage.

She passed an info card, and I slid it into my back pocket.

"Small groups are crucial to engage our faith in Jesus. We're really encouraging people to plug in."

"Thank you. I'll look into it." I lied, and she seemed to notice. I doubt she intended to, but she assessed me, head to toe. My hair was disheveled, my brow sweaty, and—oh shit—I hadn't aimed for impropriety but I wasn't wearing a bra. I hid my pseudovisible nipple with the coffee cup.

"What neighborhood are you in? I can plug you into a local small group right now."

I wanted to scream at the top of my lungs. I wanted to tell her that—despite my appearance—I knew the Bible back and forth and upside down. "I've been to a hundred thousand small groups," I wanted to shout.

My body, meanwhile, couldn't hide her disdain. She shook. "I told you we shoulda left."

Sensing a Jezebel in peril, the nice woman frowned. "Would you like to walk in together?" She reached out her hand and it appeared to move in slow motion, like when you watch the playback of a car crash. "I'll carry your coffee."

I yanked the cup away and pulled the helmet from my bag. "I actually forgot something at home." It took self-restraint to not add a "fuck you."

While I biked to Silver Lake, I was stunned by my behavior. I decided to stay away from church for a while—for my sake and for the sake of the yellow-shirted lady. Fancying myself too broken for church, guilt gnawed at me. But I was honoring my body and I didn't even know it yet. My body remembered my trauma, she set her alarms, and—when I was in danger—she told me to run. I tried to drag her into that auditorium, kicking and screaming, into the reverberating voices of The Antagonist, but we were too raw for that and she knew it.

Finding my identity in evangelicalism was no longer a possibility. I wouldn't be accepted into that auditorium as a sexually active woman anyway. So be it.

When I returned home, I found Chelsea huddled on the couch with her cute, new boyfriend. They looked blissed out and serene. "Hi, Brenzy." I was enveloped by Tiny's love. My home was a safe haven.

Her man, Robbie, stood up and headed to the kitchen. "Could I get you anything?"

"Sparkling water?" I'd gone to church seeking the Prince of Peace but maybe I needed a Prince Charming. Purity culture sold me both. One was the savior; the other, a knight in shining armor.

"God," I prayed, "maybe a boyfriend could heal me? Maybe a man could bring me back to you."

A common belief was that church boys were safe to date, but evangelical guys freaked me out. In their attempted abstinence from sex and masturbation, they might as well have carried engagement rings in their back pockets. Church men were so desperate for "sinless" sex that those horny dates moved too fast—not physically but toward the goal of marriage.

Evangelicals are encouraged to make lists of important questions, like "How many kids do you want?" Or, "Would you be open to moving from LA?" Knowing what you want can be a positive thing, but in "courtship dating"—as it's called—it's lustful, sinful, and selfish to date someone you're not positive you could marry. On a first date, over caramel macchiatos and cake pops, the objective is to figure out if this girl is "The One." We indoctrinated Christians are not to date for the pleasure of acquainting ourselves with another soul. The girl is supposed to lean back, under the bright lights of Starbucks, and answer her date's inquisition: "I've always wanted three kids, but I'd be open to less. How many kids do you want?"

We put this pressure on teens as well. Poor fifteen-year-old kids go scratching their heads, asking, "If I entered seminary would you be willing to come with me? Is God calling you to be a pastor's wife?" This high school romance is acceptable if—and only if—it might last forever.

On the flip side, Christian guys could get horny and take women for granted. Being taught purity, not integrity, I have friends who slept with girls and never called them again because "I can't see marrying her." Men are valiant pursuers who must find "The One." In this paradigm, non-Christian women are dispensable. Like purity teachers imply, girls willing to have sex before marriage have lost their dignity anyway. Thereby, I fell into the dispensable category.

On my quest for love, I was happy to abstain if the situation required, but only for a period of time. I no longer believed that marriage is supernaturally blessed by the promise of sexual compatibility. Crack open *Pure*—Linda Kay Klein's book—and you'll know this notion to be a damaging fallacy. My trampage solidified the truth that sexual compatibility is far from simple and absolutely not guaranteed. If I dated a Christian guy, hell-bent on "saving it for marriage," I couldn't abide.

For these reasons, I wouldn't search for a boyfriend beneath the steeple.

Pastor Everyman said that dating non-Christians would drag the faithful down. When evangelicals hit it off—or even fell in love—with non-Christians, they'd be shamed and pressured into breaking up. Such connections were called unevenly yoked, based on 2 Corinthians 6:14: "Do not be yoked together with unbelievers. For what do righteousness and wickedness have in common? Or what fellowship can light have with darkness?" "Missionary dating" was frowned upon, but that's what I planned to do.

Out from underneath the steeple, I'd allow myself to date whomever I wanted, with no concern for these restrictions. After years of indoctrination, a pressure-building, anxiety-ridden, quest for "The One" was all I knew. I thought I was inviting true love, but I didn't know the first thing about building a relationship.

The absence of sex had been my Eden. Before biting the apple of sexual activity, I pined over crushes but had no concept of a broken heart. After marriage, the serpent wrapped my arm and fed me the entire tree. I had mediocre sex, ecstatic experiences, mini-love affairs, and moments I wished to forget, but I'd yet to fall in love.

When I began to sleep around, I wanted love but found hooking up could be casual and easy. I didn't mind keeping things light. I referred to myself as "a total dude about sex."

Tiny was stunned by how easily I could let someone go. "But I thought you really liked him."

I shrugged. "He'll get over it." Of my exploits, few men intrigued me past what I could gain from their affection. I wasn't after money or provision. I wanted sex. I joked I was a succubus, sucking energy from men's loins. If you're horrified that I compared my intentions to those of a demon's, you should be. My misuse of bodies drew lower levels of sex into my life. When I wasn't being hurt by a lack of care in the aftermath of sexual activity, I was harming others. I got annoyed when men pursued me. I didn't care if I made them cry. The root of my callous attitude was in the lie that men are insatiable for sex. I thought, "Whatever. They got laid," as though men don't desire companionship, love, and respect like the rest of us.

Having ditched Purity, my sexual ethic was on the floor. I thought my desire for love would supersede my ill behavior, but when I wasn't hurting men, men were hurting me.

I buck the cliché that to receive love we must hustle, ignore companionship, and wait for the perfect man. I'm a doer, and the princess-like kick-back-and-wait philosophy wasn't going to work in my pursuit of a partner. I was desperate to find a mate, not willing to wait. True love is stabilizing, and stability was what I craved. Weary of casual sex and all its drama, I pursued a Prince Charming.

My version of the prince, mind you, was not someone you'd take home to Dad. Was he charming? God yes, and that was the problem. I fell for guys who were captivating but disappointing. Like, he's a gallery artist but he also lives with his mother. Or he's a poetry savant but he doesn't text back. To make things worse, like a magpie, I was blinded by pretty things. The men I'd pursue were so aesthetically pleasing I'd be blind to their inner ugly. Not to say people are irredeemable, but I collided with these men when we couldn't have been be more misaligned.

Girlfriends—and our gay boyfriends—pardon our exes over bottles of chardonnay. Like, "Girl, his childhood *was* traumatizing!" Or, "His ex demolished his heart!" That's why he's afraid of commitment, we say, before diagnosing the offender with whichever mental illness could rationalize his bad behavior. Selfish dudes are "bona fide sociopaths." Men who cheat are "clinical narcissists." Guys who bang tons of women are "textbook manipulators."

I'll admit, I diagnosed the men I adored. I didn't hold myself accountable for what sort of love—or lack thereof—I was willing to give or accept. I didn't believe I deserved better.

❧

In my pursuit of a Prince not-so-Charming, Will and Julian entered my life.

Will—the first man to muddle my brain—had a perfect body. He had a triangle back, long limbs, and a devious smile. If you can imagine Burt Reynolds reclining on that bearskin rug, you'd have a good sense of this guy's style vibe. Will was arrogant, entitled, and cruel. He was sexy, wealthy, and charming. He took my tender heart for a ride.

Will predated my sexual lows—like the assault or when the condom went missing inside of me. At the time, he was the first person I dated after separating from Brandon. I was technically married, though moved out and broken up, and this was a point of contention for Will. We'd have passionate sex, he'd twirl my hair in his fingers, and he'd say, "I wish you could meet my parents . . . but you're married."

The paperwork was a headache, but, "My marriage is over. For good."

He'd dip my chin and bring me in for a kiss. "Doesn't matter, baby. They won't understand." With this insurance—making me believe he'd be with me if it weren't for technicalities—I carried on with our relationship. I wanted to be his girlfriend, but I was convinced my marital status was disqualifying.

"I can't wait until your divorce is final," he'd say. "My family will love you." Will spoke in tomorrows and next weeks. He was the sort of playboy who gets you dreaming about the future. "We'll go to Hawaii next Christmas. You'll love my cousin Renee."

Will's empty promises hurt because, later, I'd mourn what could've been in lieu of what we had. We didn't have a Hawaiian vacation. What we had was a brief, tormenting relationship.

The first time we had sex, Will sweated profusely and I found his scent repelling. I became disgusted beneath the beads of sweat that formed puddles on my body. "Are you okay?" I asked. My body—whom I ignored—strongly suggested we never have sex with Will again.

After that sexual mishap, I decided I wasn't into him. I'd discarded equally attractive guys before this. My world would keep spinning.

"Let me take you to dinner," he texted. I did feel bad that our sex went so badly. Also, he was shiny and new, with rough skin and plump lips.

"Fine." Ooh wee, I got suckered in. "When?"

Will swooped me up in a cream Mini Cooper and took us to downtown LA's Church & State. By candlelight, I found him engaging and sexy. He was intelligent, witty, and self-sustained. Sure, he lived in his parents' mansion, but he didn't have to. Will was saving up for a loft in the city. "That's amazing," I said, wide-eyed and hopeful.

Will ordered for us both, as princes do. We enjoyed oysters, filet, and a chocolate soufflé. He said he lived in a Pacific Palisades house with tennis courts out back, "And peacocks on the front lawn."

"No way."

"Don't get excited. They're pain in the ass rodents. Like squirrels." Will brought a spoon to my lips. "Try a snail," he said. "I dare you." I acquiesced.

Having slept with three men aside from my husband, I felt satiated. I'd learned enough from random sex, I thought. I wanted a boyfriend.

It didn't matter that Will prodded my open wounds in lieu of protecting me. Little girls are given tales about wart-covered frogs turning into princes.

As a teen I saw Heath Ledger—a frog—hopelessly aloof until

Julia Stiles inspired him to change. In fairy tales—and *10 Things I Hate about You*—the ugly thing, whether it be a frog or a character flaw, is rehabilitated by a woman's touch. Falling for this story was easy because I didn't fancy myself a girl's girl. I didn't wear pink, and I didn't dream journal or scream when I ate Magnolia Bakery's *Sex and the City* cupcakes. But heed my warning: Wearing black and pretending to be unaffected doesn't mean you're immune to fairy tales. I didn't read romance novels, but their narrative had permeated my psyche.

Though I'd disengaged from God, I wondered if he'd sent Will to save me. While this new lover intertwined his fingers in mine, our pheromones magnetized. When we had sex in his sauna—my desire now to revel in his sweat—I imagined us together. I hoped Will would spare me the perils of LA dating, but Will was the dangerous one, seemingly incapable of being earnest. Several months into our hot-and-cold love affair, he ditched me on Valentine's Day and never called again. Having put my hope of romantic redemption into Will's slippery hands, this snub was an introduction to fresh pain. I cried until I couldn't see straight.

With Sienna and Chels, I'd diagnose Will as a sociopath. "He enjoyed my misery," I said. "He got off on telling me he'd slept with another woman but 'She was nothing like you. You're next level.'"

"He's an idiot," Sienna said. "More chardonnay?"

While he might not have been a sociopath, Will was a bonafide womanizer, leaving me for a DJ and she for another woman two weeks before their Hawaiian vacation. "He used his ex's ticket and booked a different girl," Tiny told me later. I'd dodged a philanderer but, still, the ensuing heartbreak ushered me into my aforementioned trampage.

I call this moment of extreme promiscuity "trampaging" because I was on a sexual rampage. The term is by no means demonizing, vilifying, or judging people who have sex, who are making sexual choices from a place of autonomy and respect.

Trampaging, however, ushered in hookup culture, which means that the fallout was not considered. In hookup culture, bodies become a means to an end or a vehicle for our orgasms. In the midst of this, we ignore the value of others while stifling the prompts of our bodies.

I did not deserve the bad things that befell me, but I wish I'd had a sexual ethic that supported and protected me and my precious partners, whom I took for granted.

Had I known any of this, I wouldn't have looked to Will to save my soul.

If the men I pursued were books—each relationship rich with stories—Will and Julian would be the bookends. Will was my broken heart's excuse to push trampaging to its absolute limit. Julian marked the time to level out.

Julian was a portrait of aesthetic pleasure. His body looked like something Michelangelo would have carved from marble. Beneath an alluring exterior, Julian sought magic and romance. He wanted to be an actor, and I could imagine him steering a fleet across the Indian Ocean or charging an army on horseback. If not in real life, in a movie, he could certainly pretend.

Our romance was short and tender, but bitter. If you believed in past lives, you'd think we'd been lovers before, fated to fail once more.

I met Julian in a shallow place—a club in Hollywood where people wanted to be—but we drifted deeply into one another. I drove him to Beachwood Canyon, where I lived then. We stopped at the Thai restaurant and shared forkfuls of yellow and red curry. I ordinarily hated poetry or when boys strummed their guitars for me. Such romance seemed to me like an emotional plea. But the way Julian recited poetry, from books on his nightstand, he drew me in, like a sullen fly to sweet, sweet honey. He spoke with a passion that burst from his belly.

Julian didn't live in LA, so when I flew to visit his home, my mom reminded me to be brave. "I can tell that you love him," she said. "You should tell him. Even if he doesn't feel the same, you will have been brave."

"I love you." I'd whispered the words into his ear, and the ensuing silence was deafening. I sank closer to his body, burying the pain of unrequited love.

Still, Julian felt passionately for me. When he left LA, he wanted me in his dark blue city, perusing landmarks and boarding the ferry to Victoria Island. We intertwined our bodies in the seats, wrapping limbs over limbs insatiably. When we were in private, I couldn't talk long before Julian would begin again, undressing me and unifying our bodies. We were in ecstasy.

Love arrives with no assurance of safety. As a matter of fact, falling in love might be the most dangerous thing I'd ever done. And I knew why they called it "falling." Before I boarded the plane to visit Julian, I stood on the precipice of indecision. When I fell for him, I'd decided to take that leap. But when I fell, Julian's arms weren't prepared to catch me. When he and I visited my friend Stacey at her parents' home in Victoria, her mom said Julian seemed "full of shit." My darling friend and her mom feared Julian's romantic lean. They didn't trust him and, like most people with a bird's eye, perhaps they were right not to.

I was raised to fear heartbreak, believing that losing a lover would make me irrevocably diminished or less than, but it wasn't like what Purity had said. Falling in love was a gain and a loss, in solidarity. I'd lost the man who introduced me to love, but I was richer and wiser for it. For better or worse, love changes and expands us. I was proud to have taken that leap.

By the time Julian hurt me, my soul had expanded. I had fallen in love for the first time. "My heart actually hurts," I told Sienna.

Before this, my heart had been a rose, restrained, my ribs its ivory cage. In Julian's presence, the petals fluttered open, pressing against my chest, pushing out, reaching for my lover.

Though Stacey's mom had been right—Julian and I wouldn't last—falling in love had not been in vain. Julian had inspired the bloom, but my heart, now open, would not return to its former dimensions.

14

SATYR

I found it sexy and endearing to hear of Julian's former pursuits. It turned me on to imagine how women would fawn, and I took pleasure in knowing that he was mine.

But, "My worst fear is to marry a whore," he said.

My gaze darted from Julian's eyes to the table, a shame response. Everyone I knew was sexually active, but men, I noticed, wanted to pretend they were my first experience. They knew better, of course, being that I was a divorcee. Still, they'd clasp hands over their ears and shout, "La, la, la!" if I shared a sex story. Because of this, I'd resigned myself to the belief that I'd have to keep my trampage under lock and key. "What do you mean?"

"I don't want to marry a whore."

This man wasn't my boyfriend, but I was madly in love. I was afraid to lose him. "You mean, you wouldn't marry a woman who has sex for money?"

Julian paused and regarded me coldly. "I mean, I wouldn't marry a whore."

I bit my lip and continued eating. When Julian said "whore" he meant me.

It was true: I'd slept with whomever I wanted, for my pleasure or to my detriment. But Julian's affection had pulled me, willingly, toward monogamy. Sure, I couldn't share my past, but I could forgive myself and emerge a saint. I wanted to be Julian's Madonna. After all, he wouldn't accept a whore.

Early in our love affair, Julian explained that he was familiar with sex workers. His father owned a row of strip clubs where he grew up. "The strippers introduced me to everything," he said. "Carnal knowledge." His voice seemed unfamiliar, absent of its usual gentleness and poetry. I wondered if Julian had been sexually assaulted.

I know a handful of men whose stories of sexual debut involve their mom's friend, or a babysitter, or their dad egging them on to "get laid." Little Wayne brags on being peer pressured into having sex at eleven. Which all begs the question, do gender scripts—about teen boys' supposed horniness—justify the predatory behavior of these adults? Did Julian's dad offer him a dancer before he was willing or able to consent?

I was sorry to intuit this trauma, but where did it leave us? Regardless of Julian's past, he'd called me a whore. He considered me less.

This fateful dinner conversation became one of our last.

In the midst of my and Julian's breakup, Sienna dragged me to Joshua Tree. And—at the risk of sounding new-age and hippie-dippie—let's be honest: The desert is a restorative place. The Joshua trees spring from the ground, sturdy and warm beneath a blanket of sparkling, iridescent stars. At home in LA, the smog and city lights obstruct our view of the cosmos, but in the desert God's majesty is on display.

Sienna and I climbed the boulders, topless and alone beneath the kiss of hot sun. My skin turned pink, and we took a few shots for my Instagram. The posts, showing me in a baby blue bikini, arms up, booty popped, were meant to say, I'm fine!, though, of course, I wasn't. I wept hot tears onto Sienna's soft shoulder. "Let's throw a party at your place," she suggested. At this point, I shared a craftsman in Beachwood with three girlfriends.

When Sienna and I pulled into the drive, she clapped her hands together. "This will be delightful, honey. I promise." She'd suggested that I ring Julian's friends and invite them over. For better or worse, she knew how to get under an ex lover's skin. Revenge, however, wasn't my motivation. Julian admitted he'd fallen in love with another woman, far north. His LA friends were my lingering connection to him.

Not realizing how brokenhearted I was, how desperately I needed healing, I went tumbling into a relationship with Julian's friend. When Sienna and I trotted down the hall with a fresh bottle of mescal, Lex was sitting on the couch beside my housemate Cat. "Woo," Cat sang. "Pour me some of that."

Lex obliged. We caught eyes.

Have you heard the Middle Ages legend of the Pied Piper? The story goes that a rat catcher, hired by a rodent-infested city, was to lure their pests away. The Piper would blow into a magic whistle and the rats would follow wherever the Piper went, straight out of the city.

I myself knew a Pied Piper. He had greasy, black hair and possessed an abounding trust fund. The whistle he blew was the ding of a text message announcing that he had teeny plastic bags filled with cocaine. Ding! Rats would scurry from the dark ends of LA and follow the Piper to whichever club he went. He led them to Teddy's and then to his house, where they'd party to the redundant noise of trance music. Overstaying their welcome, the rats would move into the Piper's home and snort up the Piper's fortune.

Referring to a man and his friends as rats is judgmental, if not cruel. But I've been honest thus far. I'm imperfect, and I admittedly grew to hate these boys. They had unprotected sex and refused to pay for the abortions they demanded. The rats were addicts and fiends, taking for granted anyone who crossed their path. They'd claw a girlfriend's hair until she screamed; they'd tussle in the foyer over a missing bag of ketamine.

Once, I saw a girl lost in a K-hole. The Piper had treated us to a late-night meal at Café 101, but when the girl disappeared, he insisted we leave her to fend for herself. I worried she'd be lost, wandering the streets of Hollywood. "Please," I said, "her purse and phone are here."

The Piper curled the end of his stringy hair and drew close to my face. "Fuck her," he said. To the rats, "Let's go."

And, horrifying as it may be, I got into the Piper's car. I gripped the girl's purse, with tears in my eyes, but I was too weak. I didn't want my new boyfriend Lex to leave me.

Abusive relationships are insidious. Many of us were raised to believe that abuse comes in the form of hits and closed fists. If you're not being slapped or punched, it's conceivable your relationship is normal. On television, and at the police station, the victims of abuse are sporting black eyes or the scars of cigarette burns. Physical abuse is awful, no doubt, but what people don't realize is that abuse increases in intensity, slowly, over a long period of time.

I've tried to figure out how I entered—and stayed in—an abusive relationship. This romance with Lex is perplexing and a source of deep shame. When people point to my tattoo—the tattoo Lex gave me—I shudder and hide it away. "I'll talk about anything," I'll say. "Sex, drugs, poo, anything but my tattoos." Friends and strangers respectfully don't press the issue.

"It's beautiful, though," my partner David said, gently pulling up my top for a better view of the peacock feather on my ribs.

"I hate it." It wasn't until this playful evening with my current partner that I realized why. "It reminds me of how low I went. How willing I was to disrespect my body. My ex made a mark on me forever. And it's ugly."

David thought for a moment. "The most hopeful part of you wanted to heal a broken person. And you couldn't. You loved someone. That's nothing to be ashamed of."

My lip quivered while I flung a sweater over the grotesque stain of ink. "I'll work on forgiving myself," I promised.

"You should," he said. "You didn't do anything wrong." But that statement wasn't entirely true.

Perhaps it wasn't my fault that Julian had broken my heart and propelled me into Lex's arms. Perhaps it wasn't my fault that Lex somehow kept me from family and friends, convincing me I was foolish and dull, incapable of doing better than settling for the scraps of himself. I sought compassion for this former version of myself, but she had done awful things. In her obsession with Lex's affection, she let another woman roam the streets of Hollywood, vulnerable, alone, and fucked up on ketamine. The girl turned up at my Beachwood place the next morning, saying a neighbor found her—blacked out—on his stoop. "I guess I slept on his couch," she said sheepishly. "Thanks for holding my purse."

Another time, Lex had sex with a girl on the Piper's bathroom floor. When she got pregnant, I watched him agonize until she opted for an abortion. I stayed silent, advocating for her only when he refused to pay half. "You need to drive her to the clinic and help. It's your fault." That night, he held me in bed, saying he wished it were me who'd gotten pregnant.

Lex pushed the girl into an abortion by promising her he'd be a garbage father. I doubt I could have intervened and changed that story, but I despise a complacent bystander.

Mom and I were once watching a movie where a murderer leapt from his pickup truck to strangle a young girl on a bicycle. The murder itself was deplorable, but it was the man sitting in the passenger seat of the truck, watching, unmoved, while the girl is murdered that made me want to hurl.

Like this, I witnessed the Pied Piper and his rats plunder the town, inhaling drugs like their noses were minivacs. I said nothing.

My girlfriend was flung around the Pied Piper's bedroom, physically abused into an abortion of her own. When she stood at the doorframe, teary-eyed, searching my face for compassion, I didn't notice. I was busy chasing Lex around the Chateau house, scurrying around with the other rats.

Unwilling to face these moments head on, I'm not writing you from an entirely healed place. Still, it's important that I grant this former Brenda compassion. Not only because she's a part of me but because you may be trapped in a relationship like hers. Maybe you've loved someone who—like Lex—became a personification of The Antagonist. Maybe you've heard that you're worthless, unworthy, and not that interesting or special. Maybe, by the time someone came along and abused you, you were primed to believe you deserved it.

When Lex promised I couldn't find anyone better, Julian's words rang through my ears. "My worst fear is to marry a whore." Julian was wonderful, I thought, and he'd never marry a whore. Maybe no one would.

I lived like this for a couple years, scurrying with Lex and the rats. I modeled and the clients took notice of my dimming light. "Are you all right?" my agent would ask. I spent hours chasing Lex's affection, scared he'd fall between another pair of legs. Bags appeared beneath my eyes. I dyed my hair blood red from a box.

I wanted to protect Lex and myself in equal measure. I bought him alcohol but poured it in moderation. I'd convince him to leave the Piper's house and hole up with me at his parents' place outside of LA. When we were away, I felt safe. These were the redeeming moments, when he'd talk as if he loved me. We'd make art with puffy paint and cruise the streets of Palm Springs, going ten miles per hour in a golf cart. I thought if I could keep him away from the darkness we could ascend to the light. He was addicted to self-destruction, but the desert kept him at bay, and there I could breathe.

If you asked me why I was so dang captivated by Lex, I'd be hard-pressed to offer a satisfying response. I suppose I saw a frog, with kind eyes and a mound of potential. Lex was a talented painter but never had the work ethic to pursue art. His work was complicated and intuitive, made of ink prints and found objects. In my Beachwood hall, he stored a magnificent Adam and Eve painting. I thought, "He knows God." Or at least, he used to. His first tattoo read "Magdalene." Lex explained that he had an adoration for Mary Magdalene and that he believed she'd been Jesus's lover.

Beyond his talent, which I'll admit I fetishized, I found a means to excuse his sins. When he shared a hint of childhood trauma, I satisfied myself with those stories, finding his past an apt excuse for bad behavior.

And if you're wondering: Yes, my housemates despised him. The girls could recognize a wreck and the tension in our home intensified. One girl moved out and was replaced by Cat's boyfriend, Bryan, and his friend Troy. Lex continued his antics, and after a while I didn't say hi to my evasive housemates, annoyed by their judgment. I apologized profusely for Lex's bad behavior, but no one would forgive him. I resented my housemates for shaming me when really I was ashamed of myself. Cat and Bryan were exhausted, privy to my abusive relationship. "You're so bright and beautiful without Lex," Bryan said.

One night, Lex and the Piper scurried though the house, breaking glasses and starting a fight. The household chose sides, myself and Lex versus everyone else.

Alienated and embarrassed, I began looking for an apartment of my own.

Cat stacked her wood, spray paints, and art supplies on the front porch. She was an incredible talent, repurposing fallen plumage and dried driftwood into intricate art. At this time, she had joined her boyfriend Bryan, a traveling musician, on his American tour. Sara was the only housemate who still spoke to me, but she was also away, visiting family in Nashville. I had a white bunny for a pet, named Monroe, and she hopped around the house with Cat's two pups. The bright, light energy of the animals was our only source of collective joy. I knelt down to pet Cat's sweet pit and took solace in that fact that everyone but Troy was gone.

Troy and I often ignored each other, his disdain for me apparent, so when we passed each other in the hall our silence was nothing new. I was off to shoot a video on Catalina Island.

After years of modeling, I'd acquired a beautiful wardrobe. Most dresses I owned were sewn to fit to my body. I possessed custom-made leather jackets and vintage furs. I cherished silk lingerie pieces that were family heirlooms. I passed on these items, however, and chose ill-fitting blouses and beat-up sneakers to throw in my carry-on to Catalina. I would be playing a girl experiencing a metamorphosis, and the director intended to show this transformation through my attire. "Think ugly," he'd instructed. "Wardrobe will provide the 'after' clothes, so think 'before.'" I crashed down the front stairs with a suitcase full of junk.

"You have everything?" Lex asked. He was taking me to dinner—on my dime—before I drove to the Long Beach pier to catch the ferry.

"Yep. All packed." I threw my luggage into the trunk.

"I forgot my keys," he said. "One sec," and in a few moments, Lex returned, asking what would become a crucial question. "You want your bedroom door open or shut?" My bunny Monroe had free rein of the house, but sometimes I liked to keep her confined to my room.

In my absence, I thought, she'd want company. "Leave it open."

Lex and I headed downtown for drinks.

A few hours later, I was pulling into the Long Beach pier when Troy rang my phone. For someone who may have hated me, this call was unusual. "Hello?"

"Hey, Bren. Are you driving? Can you pull over?"

My thoughts went to Monroe. Was she dead? Injured? I found a parking space and yanked the car's brake. "Is everything okay?"

There was a bit of silence, and then, "The house is on fire."

I begged him to explain in more detail, the scope of the fire, the damage, but he insisted I come home and see. The vague implication was that the oven was in flames.

"Monroe's all right," he said. Troy was stoic and difficult to read.

As I crawled down the 405 in rush-hour traffic, my stomach twisted in knots. An unfamiliar number rang my phone. "Hello?"

"Brenda? This is your neighbor. I've got Monroe with me."

My heart stopped. We never talked to our neighbors. Who was this? "You do?"

"She's in pretty bad shape. I need your permission to bring her to the hospital."

"What?" I wished my car had wings so I could soar over the bumper-to-bumper traffic.

"Honey, stay calm," she said. "I'm going to bring your bunny to the hospital if that's okay?"

"Wait, what?" The tears began to flow. "How bad is she?"

Instead of an answer, she said, "How soon can you be here?"

I called my parents for a prayer.

I know I haven't mentioned Jesus in a bit, but I did speak to him, all the time. I couldn't help it. Since childhood, Jesus was my solace. I couldn't deny that I felt his presence, even when I didn't believe I deserved his love.

Nearing the house, getting closer now, a tornado of smoke rose into the sky. Firetrucks blocked my path, so I parked in the middle of the street and went running. When I saw the house, my knees buckled and I fell to the ground. My bedroom, which was in the front of the house, looked like a cartoon mouse hole, black and vacant. Troy appeared and lifted me up from the asphalt.

"Where's Monroe?"

"Right here." The kind neighbor, a woman adorned with turquoise and silver jewelry, passed a plastic container to me. My little companion sat inside, her white fur and perfect black eyeliner bloody and burnt to a crisp. Monroe was trembling and covered in soot; her feet were swollen and raw.

People were talking to me, but I couldn't hear their voices. A fireman asked the last time I'd seen fire and I answered honestly, "I burnt sage." This statement would get me unofficially blamed for the fire by my landlord and housemates, but had I really burnt the place down? Determining fault was more complicated than that.

Monroe's hay was potent, so I'd light sage to mask her scent. Town gossips would hear "sage" and say that we were a house of mad witches who'd been performing a ritual. This was untrue, of course, but you might argue that my housemates and I were the catalyst somehow, like sticks rubbing together. Tension sparked, and our collective anger burst into a flame.

It was fire season and I'd burned sage. Neighbors walked by and smoked cigarettes. Cat's art supplies themselves were a pyre on the porch. Troy said he'd heard the POP! POP! POP! of Cat's spray cans exploding before he'd noticed the flames.

Someone had called Tiny, and she ran to me in the street. "Oh my God, Bren." She peered into the plastic container. "You have to get Monroe to the vet."

"We're going." Lex led me to his truck and buckled us in, tenderly. He was showing the compassion I desperately needed, and I soaked it up.

Once we arrived at the animal hospital, my memory blurs. The

vet had told us that Monroe's little lungs, full of smoke, would de-
cay over time. "They degrade. Do you understand?"

"I understand." I leaned into Monroe's cage before they placed
her in an incubator. "Don't die on me, babe," I said. "You're all I've
got." Then I bade her farewell.

That night, Tiny, Lex, and I shared a bottle of wine at La Pou-
belle. I leaned on my arms, exhausted, having run out of tears.
"Monroe's gonna make it," Chelsea said. "I promise." My abusive
relationship had transformed me into an absent, shitty friend, but
Tiny was more like a sister. She loved me unconditionally.

In the morning, someplace in the scorching hot Valley, I lay in
Lex's bed. Eyes puffy and red, I stared at my phone, waiting for it
to ring.

"Hello?"

"I can't believe I'm telling you this."

"Yes?"

"You've got a live bunny," the vet said. "Come and pick her
up."

I brought Monroe back to Lex's, my account drained by the
hospital bill.

Lex usually behaved as though everything were an inconve-
nience, but this time his attitude improved. He read the small
labels on each medicine box so I could dose Monroe and slather
her in cream. She was a fighter, that little fur babe, apparently hiding in the back room of the house, burning her toes in the flames.
"I wish I knew which firefighter saved her."

"Why? So you could fuck him?" Lex said.

I rolled my eyes, unable to deal with his nonsense in the midst of
my plight. I had two pairs of underwear, one bra, and a bag stuffed
with clothes that I hated. Had I known my belongings would become ashes, I would've packed a very different pile of things.

I was grateful, though, that I'd told Lex to leave the bedroom
door open. Had I said, "Close it," I'd be weeping over the death

of my bunny. I thanked God that the other animals were safe and that no one had gotten hurt.

"Do you think it's my fault?" I asked Lex. He'd suffered a loss too, three of his paintings reduced to a pile of charred wood on our Beachwood lawn.

"I did it," he said.

I gazed at him, annoyed. I couldn't tell if he was joking.

15

INDECISION

There's an invitation in reflection, to dig up the past and to sift memories for their meaning. Memory lane is a pleasure, and I meander it happily, even to visit the bittersweet.

My time with Lex, however, is different. On the path through our memories, the forest grows thicker. Branches jut into my gut as I shield my face from the thicket. When friends invite me to walk the path, holding my hand, their tenderness can't protect me from the undergrowth. I come out bleeding each time, shouting profanity and being wretchedly ashamed.

Emily, my friend from *Sin Bin* days, was the one to convince me I was being abused—though many friends before her had tried, especially Sienna.

One afternoon, during a teary call, Emily asked that I look up the emotional abuse checklist. "Just google it. You'll see." When I acquiesced and took the quiz, I answered yes to questions like,

> Do you feel overpowered by your partner's presence whether or not he or she is with you?
> Do you speak carefully, or avoid speaking, so you won't risk upsetting your partner?
> Do you feel inadequate doing tasks you used to do easily?

The final question regarded children.

Does your partner control your interactions with your children or have they jeopardized their safety?

I answered no, having no children, but then I realized, "Yes."

On an emotional abuse checklist, I answered yes to forty-one of forty-one questions. This had been like the most depressing Cosmo quiz of all time, the result reading: "Girl, your boyfriend is abusing the sh*t out of you. Run!"

On the rare nights Lex gave me his blessing to leave the house, I'd blast music in the car and pretend that I was free. I didn't comprehend the grip he had on me, only knowing that if I didn't hold my phone close, ready to answer at any time, I would be subject to an argument. No matter how far I traveled, I remained tethered to my abuser.

The people I loved exercised infinite patience with me, and I missed them dearly. I didn't understand why Lex kept me isolated, but I knew it wouldn't be worth begging to see anyone—male friends, especially. After a while, I'd become a liar, to protect Lex.

"I'm too sleepy."

"I don't feel well."

"I'm in the mood to stay in."

Georgie would pout, "You don't ever come out." She missed me, of course, and Sienna spread word that Lex was deplorable. "I understand why you love him," Georgie said. "But if he's hurting you, you have to tell me."

David and Marco asked, "Is he treating you well?" I denied how bad things had gotten.

When Lisa invited me for drinks, Lex would coax me out of leaving, holding me to a suggestion I'd made a week ago. "You said we'd stay in this weekend. It's Saturday."

"I didn't know it was Lisa's birthday."

"But you promised." Lex berated me for being forgetful and for not honoring my word. "It's just fucked up you didn't tell me sooner, but go if you want to." This offer wasn't sincere, of course. If I went to the party, I'd stare at my phone, scared that if he texted I'd take too long to text back. Then I'd be in a fight, defending my fidelity.

Lex, like Julian, was petrified of shacking up with a "whore." Still, Lex, a serial abuser, was attracted to sex kittens and sex workers and Jezebels and "whores." He'd simply degrade us for who we are, or who we once were.

I was once vibrant and unafraid, but now I couldn't tell a story without Lex breathing down my neck. He said I talked and laughed too loudly. Lex humiliated me too. At comedy shows he'd heckle the performers because he was jealous of their success. Sienna's boyfriend invited us to the premiere of his feature film, and Lex slept in the front row, in full view of the esteemed cast. At the afterparty he told people he'd never marry me, and Sienna couldn't contain herself. "He's an idiot," she said. We rarely spoke after this. When we did, she'd answer in single syllables.

"Yep."

"Nope."

"Cool."

I'd lost relationships with everyone I loved.

Abusive people isolate you from family and friends. When Lex and I were alone, there were no dissenting voices. We could pretend our union was not a living hell. I clung to the few moments of Lex's tenderness, or "love bombing," as they call it. Lex bought me flowers . . . once. He built an art studio on the side of our house. "This is for you," he said. Of course, he's the artist. The studio was for him.

In the midst of my loneliness and anxiety and overwhelming shame, my period didn't arrive. Shit. I took a pregnancy test and there it was: a plus.

When Lex returned from work, I told him the news and he proposed an abortion. "You're not gonna keep it, right?"

When I was fifteen, in art class, I'd made a papier-mâché

woman, nine months pregnant, holding a gun to her belly. I called it Abortion. Everyone in school knew I was a hardcore Christian, and this project was par for the course. "It's intense," my art teacher said, her brow furrowed with concern. I could see she was worried, but I couldn't imagine why. Abortion was a sin. My opinion would never waver.

Getting older, however, hearing from the women in my life who'd had terminations, the topic became more complex. Women weren't getting abortions because they "felt like it" or as a means of birth control. Their relationships were fraught with difficulties and their emotions raw.

Still, I'd never have an abortion because God carries us through adversity. Matthew 6:26 says: "Look at the birds of the air, for they neither sow nor reap nor gather into barns; yet your heavenly Father feeds them. Are you not of more value than they?" I knew God's provision. Even from the house fire I'd emerged like a phoenix, acquiring more beautiful clothing and objects than I'd had before.

What I'd intuited since childhood was that God is good. Tragedy ensues, but God provides. The strongest people I knew were survivors and single parents. Tenacity abounds in the human spirit.

"I'm not having an abortion," I told Lex. "Never."

Every. Single. Day. Lex said, "We shouldn't do this." We aren't ready for a baby, he said. "It'll ruin your career."

Lex was the baby ruining my career. What career anyway? I was stuck at home, shrinking, becoming small to appease him. If I had a baby, I'd lose my jobs, that was true. Modeling required that I remain a specific measurement. A growing belly would disqualify me from my current work. But Lex said, "I won't support you."

So I busied myself with budgeting and researching unemployment. Pragmatism is not a quality of mine, but I would need to try. These thoughts were spinning through my mind when I knocked on my neighbor's door.

"What?"

She had one of those screens where the person can see out but you can't see in. "Hi. My name is Brenda. I'm from next door."

"I know."

"I can't see you. Do you mind open—"

"This is fine." I could hear a baby cooing on her hip and faintly see their outline.

The evening before, Lex had invited the Piper over for a drink. Their debauchery devolved to snorting lines and blasting music on the patio. I tossed and turned in the bedroom, sitting up when I heard the Piper yell, "Cunt!" My neighbor was a new mother, alone and exhausted. She'd asked them to please quiet down.

"Cunt?" She began yelling obscenities and the Piper piped back. I masked their voices by burrowing my head into a pillow. This was hell, I was sure of it.

Now, I stood at the new mother's door bearing a bottle of wine. She might have been breast feeding. I hadn't thought of this.

"I just wanted to apologize for last night."

"I'm gonna tell you something," she said while acquiescing and opening the door. I met her baby's eyes and he brightened with joy. My instinct was to coo happily but she moved him further away, as though protecting her baby from me. "You're being abused."

What? "Excuse me?"

"I don't know you. I don't care. But you are. You're being abused."

"Okay, well—"

She backed away and shut the door. Bitch!

She'd offered information I was not prepared to receive. I decided she was sleep-deprived. I once heard her screaming at her ex. She was a bitch indeed. Lex was avant-garde and his friends were assholes, but abusive? Come on.

While I prepared to become a mom, Georgie recommended I see our friend Kelsey, a single mother of two. Kels toured me around her house, showing me baby items and relaying their prices. "Babies need so little at first," she said. "Just breastmilk or formula, a crib, and a shitload of diapers." She mentioned that, being a single mom, having her family close by was essential. "I don't know what I'd do without them," she said. "What's your budget for childcare?"

"I'm not sure." I was ashamed to admit I lived month to month, without savings. I confessed that Lex planned to bail.

"You might have to move home if you have this baby. For the help. Would you be okay with that?"

If I have this baby? There had never been an if.

"Will you keep your job?"

"Well, I'll be fired. It's a modeling job."

"So, unemployment?"

"I'm self-employed so . . . I'm not eligible."

"Do you have health insurance?"

I didn't.

"Birth can be, like, six to fifty thousand dollars. Just depends whether you wind up having a vaginal birth or a C-section. Have you thought about that?"

I had not.

Each morning I leaned over the toilet. The room spun but nothing would come up. I was holding onto my insides, feeling the knock of a daughter on my vaginal door. I knew she was a girl.

"Say you're not having it," Lex said. "Tell me." I was three weeks pregnant when Lex flung open the shower curtain and hurled towels at my head. "You're killing me!"

This time, I was able to scream, like a lioness, and demand he get out. Lex ducked through the door like a scolded chihuahua.

Before this, he'd pretended to be kind. He expressed that he was patient and that having a baby would be my choice. "I'm not sure I'll be there though."

Now, leaving me to weep in the shower, he'd found a new tactic. He would try to abuse me into an abortion.

A mere week before discovering I was pregnant, I'd bought myself a convertible with money I'd saved up. I noted the backseats had child-safety labeling. I could keep my baby and my dream car, I thought. This was meant to be. I imagined my girl and me, driving down the Pacific Coast Highway with the wind in our hair.

Our friends Andy and Tegan came to see the car after I'd found out I was pregnant. This couple became my sole reprieve from Lex's abuse. Andy and Lex would smoke weed cheerfully, and I had Tegan's ear. She was the only girlfriend I could spend time with without Lex harping on me. "Hi, lovers!"

"This car is sick," Andy said.

"Sick, Bren," Tegan echoed. She and Andy were an inseparable pair, svelte with cascading waves of light brown hair—the both of them.

We decided to drive the convertible to Venice that night. I readied myself in the bathroom, intending to keep the pregnancy a secret. I wanted a night off from the agony of indecision. When we piled into the car, Lex offered to drive. Unbeknownst to me, though, he'd downed nearly a half bottle of vodka.

In Los Feliz, Lex blew through a red light. Tegan screamed when we narrowly missed being hit by an SUV. I grabbed my belly and said, "Slow down," but the words emerged as a whisper. Lex and I had been arguing that day. I grew sick and wound up losing my voice.

Tegan yanked Andy's sleeve. "Tell Lex to slow down. He's scaring us." Lex ignored Andy and sped through the back streets of Hollywood. On the freeway, he changed lanes and took his hands off the steering wheel.

"Yo, man," Andy said, grabbing the wheel. "Be careful." Lex paid no attention.

When we arrived in Venice, Lex pulled off the street, blew the sidewalk, and crashed onto the sand. "We're here!"

"Asshole!" I tried to scream, but nothing came out.

Tegan held my arm, "You okay?"

"He's trying to prove it." My words were an indistinguishable whisper. I lifted myself out of the car and onto the sand. "You're trying to prove it!" It was a nightmare, being unable to speak. Andy and Tegan stared at me helplessly. Finally, "He's trying to prove it. That he'll be a terrible father."

"You're pregnant?" Tegan sighed and met me on the sand.

⸻

To sin is to cause harm. Ceasing life is an act of harm for which there is no turning back. Therefore, by the definition I've given, abortion is a sin.

Arguably, it may be accurate to call abortion murder. But murder is the unlawful premeditated killing of another human being. Therefore, the debate revolves around legality and personhood. Regarding the former, laws vary by state. Liberal places, like California, prop up clinics while conservative places, like Alabama, tear them down. As for the latter issue of personhood, some believe that life begins at conception while others believe life is marked by a baby's first breath. "And the Lord God formed man of the dust of the ground, and breathed into his nostrils the breath of life; and man became a living soul," says Genesis 2:7. In Exodus 21, if a man causes a miscarriage he is fined, but if the woman dies he is put to death. In biblical times, the killing of a fetus wasn't classified as a capital offense.

I do not believe that the abortion debate can be won or lost, so to speak. There is always a loss, of course. But when it comes to a woman's autonomy, it is impossible to humanely restrict her. Even the strictest of Christians, for example, concede that a victim of rape or incest shouldn't be required to carry out that pregnancy. Though some do argue that the victim shouldn't compound her rapist's sin by "committing a sin of her own." Considering the trauma of sexual violence, however, this argument is widely considered to be cruel.

There is also the matter of risk and disease. Most of us agree that a terminally ill fetus shouldn't be born to suffer and die. We also broadly agree that the mother's life should be prioritized in the case of a high-risk pregnancy. No matter how often Christians refer to abortion as a black-and-white issue, when met with these caveats, they'll confess to seeing grey.

Legalistic believers, however, will often cling harshly to the black and white. "If the mother dies," I've heard a preacher say, "then God must have willed it." Go tell that to a grieving widower, Mr. Preacher. See if those words land like God's love.

Meanwhile, some liberals have deemed God the grand abortionist, with as many as one in four of all pregnancies ending in natural miscarriage.

Legally and religiously speaking, on abortion our society could run in circles forever—debating, debating, debating—as we have, for hundreds of years.

Then there is the uncomfortable truth. In 2014, the Guttmacher Institute reported that more than half of abortion clients report having a religious affiliation at the time of termination. More specifically, they report belonging to various Christian denominations. So, next time you're in church, look left, look right. Many of your sisters have experienced an abortion. Many of your brothers have too. Which brings us to the subject of shame.

I knew of a girl who'd gotten pregnant and was forced to "confess her sexual sin" to the congregation. Instead of celebrating the fact she'd chosen to bring forth life, her pastor shamed her while the father, her teen boyfriend, sat in the pews. As if pregnancy weren't half a man's fault. This young woman was forced to carry her baby like a scarlet letter, her head hung low, as though life weren't a magnificent gift.

Babies are a gift, indeed. Motherhood is a privilege. But without provision, women abort. Statistically, financial concern is the primary reason women choose abortion. As a matter of fact, a large portion of termination clients are mothers, afraid they'll be unable to provide for the children they already have.

Another reason women reportedly choose abortion is due to relationship woes. "This is why you ought to be married to have sex," says Pastor Everyman, and that's a valid retort. But life is messy and complex. People don't often wait for their weddings, and husbands can leave their wives too. Pregnancy renders women more vulnerable and in need of their mate. (Sorry, uber feminists: it's true.) But men, regardless of religious affiliation, aren't always up to the task.

I myself was pregnant and would be losing my job.

My boyfriend was taunting and abusing me, threatening to leave.

I held onto my belly and joked that my daughter was a vampire sucking my energy. Pregnancy produced hormones that were foreign to me. I cried on a dime. My thoughts ran slowly, as though meandering through fog. One day, I'd be a mom-to-be. The next day, I'd consider sinning.

⚜

You might say that Roger and Robin are psychics. In Christianity, you'd call them prophets. Semantics aside, they are powerful seers. My mom introduced me to this Southern couple years prior, and I called them now, begging for an answer.

"Oh, you're pregnant," Roger said. "Let me get my wife." I hadn't said more than "hello" before Roger intuited my predicament.

We'd spoken in the past about good things, like sorting through childhood trauma and pursuing far-reaching goals. Roger and Robin exercised a technique that required the removal of their personal opinions. We're still human, so this practice isn't foolproof, but they were earnest and did their best. They'd pray fervently before a session, asking the Holy Spirit to come forth and use them as vessels. This is why, when I admitted considering an abortion, they didn't flinch. Of course they objected, as grandparents and Christians. They perceived life to be a blessing and not a curse. But, "What's he like?" Robin inquired about Lex.

"He's awful," I said, sitting on the counter and kicking my legs. "He won't stay."

"And you're afraid to lose him?"

"No." I didn't yet recognize Lex as an abuser, but I knew he was a detriment to a child's well-being. "He's a terrible person. I'm scared the baby will search for a father the rest of her life."

Roger and Robin would not be invasive or tell me what to do. These prophets simply prayed with me. We wept together. "I'm sorry," Robin said. "I'm so sorry."

⚮

Emily Meade has a way of arriving in town when I need her the most. The night before, she'd asked, "Are you having it?" I nodded yes and her mouth burst into a smile. "Oh my goodness!" She'd kissed my belly.

Now, Emily would be coming to our house to meet my elusive boyfriend. Lex and I drove to the store to buy groceries for dinner.

THU-THUMP-THUMP!

"What was that?"

"A basketball," he said.

My eyes had been on the road when I saw something flash before the car. It could've been a ball, but I felt a crackling beneath the tires. "We have to check."

"Fuck, Brenda, just keep going."

Now I knew it wasn't a basketball. Lex was lying. "I'm not leaving an animal to die."

After I U-turned, Lex folded his arms in fury. "You're not gonna wanna see this," he said. I parked the car and stomped down the street, with Lex following behind me.

Outside our neighborhood bodega, a young girl crouched beside a car, reaching her hand underneath. My belly lurched. "Hello?"

The girl looked at me coldly and I peered down. "Oh, my God." A tabby cat was writhing in pain, her matted fur covered in blood. My knees hit the curb. "He's dying?"

"*She's* dying." The girl clutched her backpack and sat back. "She's a stray, but I've been feeding her."

I sat beside the girl and we gazed at the stray together. The cat's death was grotesque and excruciating. Her life was slipping away, too slowly. "It's my fault," I said. "I hit her." The girl glared at me before we both laid our hands on the tabby. I diverted my eyes as she took her final breath. When I looked down again, her spirit was gone. I had reduced her to a mound of flesh and fur. "She ran out of nowhere."

The girl stood and wiped gravel from her jeans. "Whatever," she said.

"Hold on. Let me help." I was disturbed by what I'd caused, but I couldn't process it now. "Lex?" He leaned against the wall smoking a cigarette. "Forget it." I ran into the bodega and bought trash bags. I asked if they had a spare cardboard box.

Back outside, the girl paced the pavement. She swung her backpack around, which was covered in 69 patches and little green aliens. She avoided my eyes. I needed to take care of this young one in the aftermath of her trauma. I knelt beside the cat, unraveled a trash bag, and repressed my disgust. There was excrement everywhere.

I was figuring a way to get her inside the bag when I heard Lex sigh. He nudged me aside and quickly covered the cat. He tied the bag, placed it in the cardboard box, and handed the box to the girl.

Never looking at us, she took the makeshift coffin and walked away silently.

"I told you," Lex said. "You shouldn't have stopped."

"I don't regret stopping. She needed us."

He headed back to the car. "Whatever." He was furious and, above all, inconvenienced. He had no regard for the dead animal, for the sullen girl, or for me. He didn't care about anyone.

We told Emily what had happened and Lex played along, as if he'd been valiant and given a damn. But when Emily leaned down to kiss my belly again, I stopped her. I was no longer sure I'd be having a daughter.

Planned Parenthood and the evangelical church appear to be mortal enemies. The organization is accused—by religious folk—of pushing women into abortions, but this wasn't my experience.

I have a long-time appreciation for Planned Parenthood. Because I was unable to afford insurance, they'd become my sole healthcare provider. Before I got married, I went for check-ups and to regulate my period. After marriage, they gave me free birth control because we weren't ready to have a child. On my trampage, I'd stop by for free condoms and a few tablets of Plan B. For over ten years, Planned Parenthood kept me healthy and child-free.

Now, for the first time, I was in their specific branch that dealt with tragedy.

Because this is my story, and I vowed to be honest, I won't sugarcoat how painful this can be. I've learned that some women are casual about a termination, but this reaction seems rare. To the contrary, girlfriends have spoken of regret, if not for the termination itself then for whatever led up to it. Like,

I should have been more careful.
We should have bought the Plan B.

"I'd have a four-year-old by now," a friend would say, staring into the distance, daydreaming about what might have been.

Occasionally, I've encountered women who became pregnant out of ignorance. Without comprehensive sex ed, you'd be shocked by the questions I've received. Like, "Can you get pregnant via anal sex?" or, "If I'm not ready for a baby won't my body just reject it?," the answer to both being no. (Though regarding the former, you must be cautious with semen. Fertility is a potent disposition.)

At Planned Parenthood, the staff touched me, in tenderness. The process took an entire day, from 8:00 a.m. to 6:00 p.m. Female providers shuffled me from room to room and asked three, four, five times if this was my choice. "Has anyone pressured, manipulated, or coerced you into this decision?"

"No." I turned away from the ultrasound.

Left alone in an exam room, I gripped my belly. "I'm sorry I failed you, baby." My lip trembled. "I'll rearrange my whole life so you can come back again."

In the final moments, a nurse played classical music as I breathed in the sedative. With my consciousness fading, I wept. I thought, Wait!

There was a dull pressure and I heard a swish. "We're done." Someone led me to a post-op room for juice and a cookie. I ate sullenly, pretending nothing had happened.

On the ride home I asked Lex to pull over so I could vomit. I hunched on the pavement, gagging and tearing at my gut.

At home, Lex hummed a melody. He'd gotten what he wanted.

"Thou shalt not judge." We know this verse, no matter what faith we practice, if any.

Not judging one another is the great challenge of this life. I've judged Lex for abusing me. I've judged myself for staying. I've judged a girl in Planned Parenthood's post-op for not being remorseful enough.

No matter what you've done or experienced, it is my top priority—an actual call from God—not to judge you. And I don't. If you're reading this, judging the hell out of me, I understand. I've done the same to others.

As for the morality of abortion, I have opinions that I choose not to share, because the situation is complex and—at times—inconceivable.

When I called Roger and Robin again, words didn't need to be spoken. I sat on the counter again, kicking my legs, this time sobbing in apology. "Let's pray," Roger said. Roger asked me her name.

"Rose."

"She's lingering, Brenda. She's worried about you."

I'd never heard such a thing, let alone from a Christian. Christians speak in finality, not of past or future lives.

"Is it all right if she moves on?" Roger asked. "Do you need her to stay?"

"No, Rose should be free."

"That's right. We shouldn't tether spirits to ourselves."

"I want her to come back."

"Is she free or not?"

I wept. "She's free."

I needed to uproot and destroy everything.

Purity culture's end of the pendulum's swing had perverted my sexuality; hookup culture had broken my heart and led me to sin.

In the final days, I was weak and allowed Lex to linger, but my complacency emboldened his abuse. He dragged me naked from bed and flung me across the living room. He uppercut me while I held a box of blueberries, making believe that he was kidding. Our coffeemaker shattered on the floor, and I screamed, "Get out!"

The Antagonist reared up for a field day, roaring into my ear that I was irreparably broken.

I told the voice to kiss off. Shame and fear had led me to this place. I couldn't allow The Antagonist to win anymore. I kicked Lex out and painted the apartment walls in a day.

I'd never deserve a baby or a soulmate, I thought, but God promised unconditional love. If nothing else, love was what I needed.

16

ALTAR

I was with God again, alone with nothing to lose. Fear had propelled me into evil, and evil became, not a distant idea, but something that breathed down my neck. Fear told me I'd go to hell, but he was lying, as he always does. I begged God for forgiveness, which he offered me freely.

Women who get abused, have abortions, or get their hearts broken are not evil by design. Plainly, evil is the antithesis of God, which is the antithesis of love. What we know as original sin is simply our propensity to wallow in shame and fear. Both emotions led me to harm myself and others. I discovered that "sin" was not a checklist of dos and don'ts. Sin was more complex and more simple. I needed to navigate my soul out of this mess and return to true love.

If I had sex, I decided, I'd no longer leave spirit outside. "Get in here," I'd say. "Maybe this is wrong, maybe it's right, but I need you, Holy Spirit, with me." No longer could decisions be made in the dark, with my soul and body compartmentalized.

With Purity exorcised, integrity prompted questions in me. "Does this feel right? Are you two aligned?"

When I answered no, my body lacked desire. This flesh machine with her ivory ribcage and beating heart—she was worthy. I paid attention to her. I used her finger to delete the phone numbers of men who'd treated her recklessly. When I returned to church and she screamed, I left.

God taught me to align sexuality with spirit. Together, they would thrive.

This alignment began imperfectly, of course. Piecing together a divided body, soul, and mind wouldn't happen overnight. I made out with a sadist before realizing to what extent he'd require pain. I slept with a forty-some-year-old chef who looked great on paper but wouldn't text back.

"Does this feel right?" Spirit asked. "Are you two aligned?" No.

Each experience—and there were few—drew my body back to the Divine. Soon, I was dating no one, more enthralled by connection, which was hard to come by.

I entertained one relationship in the aftermath of my abortion. Cameron, the photographer, sweat into my back, this sex poking my behind. I turned over to kiss him, my friend of six months, and he treated me generously. When a comedian on TV listed her sexual conquests, Cameron called her a whore. This was a joke, and I burst into grateful laughter. Cameron didn't believe a woman could be a whore. Maybe other men would feel the same.

Empowered by love and Christlike alignment, I traveled to Berlin. Stacey—my dear friend—put me up in her flat. She and her husband took us to gay bars where the walls were plush with pink fur. "It's the inside of a vagina," Stacey said.

"I can see that."

The final night in town, I left for Berghain. Stacey couldn't accompany me to the notorious night club, so I went on my own.

I waited in line in Berlin's bitter winter, with leather pants and an enormous fur coat. I sipped vodka and yerba mate from a can until the doorman let me in. He was stout and buff, like a bulldog, flanked by guards with shaved heads and chrome belt buckles.

Inside, I checked my coat. Deep trance boomed while I ascended the staircase, gripping the metal rail. I was intent on being alone but met a lovely girl in the bathroom. We were resonant, like schoolgirls on a playground. We danced from room to room, holding hands, spending the night together. We didn't judge one another for dancing at a sex club in Berlin.

This is just like me, I thought, while spinning across the floor.

I craved adventure but just anything wouldn't cut it anymore. I promised authenticity. I devoted myself to not harming others. I'd fail, in my God-given humanity, but I'd stay awake. Love—the savior within me—was too important to neglect.

In this gigantic warehouse, stacked with dance floors and a dungeon, the girl and I wound up at an altar. A church had been gutted and repurposed, the pulpit holding not a priest, but a DJ.

There, standing atop a sex dungeon, before the altar of God, I prayed for my future baby. I apologized for Rose, but it was finished. I lifted my arms, like I had in the beginning, in a church where Purity had gotten a hold of me. Released now from his wicked grasp, I found the safest altar I'd ever prayed at in the belly of a nightclub. I smiled, and God whispered a piece of true romance. Romans 8:38–39: "For I am persuaded that neither death, nor life, nor angels, nor principalities, nor powers, nor things present, nor things to come, nor height, nor depth, nor any other creature, shall be able to separate us from the love of God."

EPILOGUE

December 18, 2019, my son, Valentine, burst into this place and drew his first breath. He cried on my chest.

I told him life wouldn't be easy but that he's inherently good, worthy of love, and welcome to love whoever he loves.

I pray the same for you and for those you raise or mentor. May we keep our young ones from fear and shame, for each generation to come.

RECOMMENDED RESOURCES

Sex

Bolz Weber, Nadia. *Shameless*. New York: Convergent Books, 2019.

Finch, Jamie Lee. *You Are Your Own: A Reckoning with the Religious Trauma of Evangelical Christianity*. Self-published, 2019.

Harris, Kat. *Sexless in the City: A Sometimes Sassy, Sometimes Painful, Always Honest Look at Dating, Desire, and Sex*. Grand Rapids: Zondervan, 2021.

Klein, Linda Kay. *Pure: Inside the Evangelical Movement That Shamed a Generation of Young Women and How I Broke Free*. New York: Atria, 2019.

Nagoski, Emily. *Come as You Are: The Surprising New Science That Will Transform Your Sex Life*. New York: Simon & Schuster, 2015.

Orenstein, Peggy. *Boys & Sex: Young Men on Hookups, Love, Porn, Consent, and Navigating the New Masculinity*. New York: Harper, 2020.

Orenstein, Peggy. *Girls & Sex: Navigating the Complicated New Landscape*. New York: Harper, 2016.

Roberts, Matthias. *Beyond Shame: Creating a Healthy Sex Life on Your Own Terms*. Minneapolis: Fortress, 2020.

LGBTQ

Beeching, Vicky. *Undivided: Coming Out, Becoming Whole, and Living Free from Shame*. New York: HarperOne, 2018.

Chu, Jeff. *Does Jesus Really Love Me? A Gay Christian's Pilgrimage in Search of God in America*. New York: Harper, 2014.

Garcia, Kevin. *Bad Theology Kills: Undoing Toxic Belief & Reclaiming Your Spiritual Authority*. Self-published, 2020.

Gushee, David P. *Changing Our Mind*, 3rd ed. Canton, MI: Read the Spirit Books, 2017.

Kegler, Rev. Emmy. *One Coin Found: How God's Love Stretches to the Margins*. Minneapolis: Fortress, 2019.

Vines, Matthew. *God and the Gay Christian: The Biblical Case in Support of Same-Sex Relationships*. New York: Convergent Books, 2015.

Biblical Interpretation

Bessey, Sarah. *Jesus Feminist: An Invitation to Revisit the Bible's View of Women*. New York: Howard, 2013.

Borg, Marcus. *Reading the Bible Again for the First Time: Taking the Bible Seriously but Not Literally*. New York: HarperOne, 2001.

Enns, Peter. *How the Bible Actually Works: In Which I Explain How an Ancient, Ambiguous, and Diverse Book Leads Us to Wisdom Rather Than Answers and Why That's Great News*. New York: HarperOne, 2019.

Evans, Rachel Held. *Inspired: Slaying Giants, Walking on Water, and Loving the Bible Again*. Nashville: Nelson, 2018.

Lewis, C. S. *The Screwtape Letters*. San Francisco: HarperSanFrancisco, 2001.

Sellers, Tina Schermer. *Sex, God, and the Conservative Church: Erasing Shame from Sexual Intimacy*. New York: Routledge, 2017.

Young, William Paul. *Eve: A Novel*. New York: Howard Books, 2015.